HEALING LIFE'S DEEPEST HURTS

Healing Life's Deepest Hurts

*Let the Light of Christ Dispel the
Darkness in Your Soul*

EDWARD M. SMITH

Regal

From Gospel Light
Ventura, California, U.S.A.

Published by Regal Books
From Gospel Light
Ventura, California, U.S.A.
Printed in the U.S.A.

Regal Books is a ministry of Gospel Light, a Christian publisher dedicated to serving the local church. We believe God's vision for Gospel Light is to provide church leaders with biblical, user-friendly materials that will help them evangelize, disciple and minister to children, youth and families.

It is our prayer that this Regal book will help you discover biblical truth for your own life and help you meet the needs of others. May God richly bless you.

For a free catalog of resources from Regal Books/Gospel Light, please call your Christian supplier or contact us at 1-800-4-GOSPEL or www.regalbooks.com.

Originally published by Servant Publications in 2002.

Portions of this book were excerpted from *Beyond Tolerable Recovery* and *Abound Training in Theophostic Ministry,* both by Edward M. Smith.

Cover design by Alan Furst, Inc., Minneapolis, Minn.

**Library of Congress Cataloging-in-Publication Data
(Applied for)**

2 3 4 5 6 7 8 9 10 11 12 13 14 15 /11 10 09 08 07 06 05 04

Rights for publishing this book in other languages are contracted by Gospel Light Worldwide, the international nonprofit ministry of Gospel Light. Gospel Light Worldwide also provides publishing and technical assistance to international publishers dedicated to producing Sunday School and Vacation Bible School curricula and books in the languages of the world. For additional information, visit www.gospellightworldwide.org; write to Gospel Light Worldwide, P.O. Box 3875, Ventura, CA 93006; or send an e-mail to info@gospellightworldwide.org.

CONTENTS

AUTHOR'S STATEMENT OF FAITH

I believe that...

- There is one God, eternally coexistent in three persons: the Father, the Son, and the Holy Spirit. The Father sent His only Son to become the redemption for lost mankind. The Holy Spirit was sent to complete the mission of Christ through His body, the Church.

- The Bible is the inspired Word of God and is "profitable for teaching, reproof, correction and training in righteousness" (2 Tm 3:16). It is timeless and relevant for all circumstances and is the fullness of God's divine inspired revelation to man, without error in its original form. Careful measure must be taken as it is interpreted by the student today to avoid rendering it incorrectly, based on a preconceived notion or previously held understanding. The Word of God must be allowed to interpret itself by itself in its accurate historical and literary context.

- Jesus Christ came in the flesh fully God and fully man, yet without sin. As God the Son, He came to earth as a man, born of a virgin, fulfilled all He was sent to accomplish, died on the cross for the sins of the world, after three days rose from the dead, and rules today at the right hand of God the Father. He will return in the clouds on the day appointed by the Father to call up all those who belong to Him who have been regenerated by the atoning work of the cross of

Christ. Jesus Christ is central to all true healing and freedom. Apart from Him we can do nothing (see Jn 15:5).

• The Holy Spirit is the Third Person of the Trinity. He lives within the heart of the true Christian, providing the power to obey God's Word, convicting of sin, teaching and leading into all truth, providing comfort in time of distress, unifying all true believers in a bond of love. The Holy Spirit is the way that God communicates with His people through opening up the written Word and through inner communication of the heart. It is the Holy Spirit who reveals truth to the person in a Theophostic Ministry session. (Even though this author sometimes uses the names Jesus, God, Spirit of Christ, and Holy Spirit interchangeably when referring to how people receive truth, he theologically believes that it is, in fact, the Holy Spirit who communicates with believers and leads them into all truth.)

• The Church is universally made up of all people who believe Jesus Christ died on the cross for their sins and rose from the dead by the power of the Heavenly Father, and through faith become partakers of the divine nature. The indwelling of the Spirit of Christ is the determining factor of one's authentic faith relationship with God, not one's denomination, religious practice, or performance in Christian disciplines. For "if anyone does not have the Spirit of Christ, he does not belong to Him" (Rom 8:9).

• The primary call and mission of the Church is to go forth and proclaim the Good News of freedom in Christ to all the world (see Mt 28:19-20), to bring truth to those held captive by the grip of the kingdom of darkness, and to prepare the way for His second coming by making ready His bride (see Lk 4:18).

* All people are born with a fallen nature separated from God. In this fallen state our hearts are separated from God and continually evil. Those who do not respond in faith to God's gracious free gift through Christ live in a fallen state and will be separated from God in an eternal hell. Those who come to Christ in faith are made new creatures and will live in heaven for all eternity. All people sin and are in need of God's continual grace and forgiveness. Sin is an ongoing problem that must be dealt with in the life of the believer through the cross of Christ and "not of works." Jesus took on our sin that we might become His righteousness. God is actively at work through the Holy Spirit in the life of the believer, renewing his mind and maturing his spirit, "till we all come to the unity of the faith and of the knowledge of the Son of God, to a perfect man, to the measure of the stature of the fullness of Christ" (Eph 4:13, NKJV).

* God is a sovereign God who is able to do "exceeding abundantly above all that we ask or think, according to the power that worketh in us" (Eph 3:20, KJV). The reason we may not experience this reality is not due to a lack of power but rather to our not appropriating the power that is available. When we seek to do ministry in our own power, nothing divine happens.

INTRODUCTION

Shari had come to talk with her pastor about the depression and anxiety that she had been experiencing over the last few months. She was already taking medication for her panic attacks, and it had helped some, yet subtle fears dogged her daily. Shari had tried to pray more, to read her Bible, and to be faithful in attending the ladies' group at her church each week, yet she was still struggling. She still entertained occasional thoughts of suicide and was in deep emotional pain.

Shari did not know it, but her pastor had just completed a video-training seminar about a new ministry approach called Theophostic Ministry. The pastor was a little uncertain as to whether he should attempt to use this approach with Shari, as he had not used it before, but he decided to at least introduce her to the approach. He began by explaining the basic principles of the ministry and then went on to help her to see why people had emotional pain such as she was having and how early childhood experiences could have an enormous impact on one's daily life. He explained to her that her panic might not be the result of a chemical imbalance but rather fearful emotions coming from a childhood experience that was being "triggered" in her present life. After listening to the pastor, Shari agreed to allow him to begin the ministry process.

The pastor prayed, asking for guidance and discernment, and then used the principles he had learned to help her follow her fear to its origin in her memory. Within a few minutes an enormous amount of pain began to surface and she began to describe a very disturbing memory of childhood abuse and emotional wounding. At times during the process the pastor did not know quite what to do and felt a little fearful himself. During these moments he would pray and review the principles in the training manual supplied at the seminar he had attended.

After a while he began to see that even though Shari was manifesting intense pain (almost as if she were actually experiencing the event she was describing), she did not seem to be out of control. He prayed softly as she walked through the entire memory, feeling all of its terror and pain. After a time he asked her to describe what she was feeling. She reported immense fear and panic (the same panic that had been surfacing in her present life). He asked her why she was feeling these emotions, and she reported that she believed she was going to die. While tempted to reassure her that she was only in a memory and was completely safe, the pastor refrained. He had learned in the seminar that this would not alleviate her fear and would only cause her to suppress it again, so he remained silent. Instead, he had her embrace the fears and encouraged her to feel them completely.

Little by little Shari came to understand and identify the true source of her pain, which was not the memory itself but the false beliefs in the memory. She said things like: "I am going to die," "I can't breathe! I'm suffocating," and "This was all my fault." In the midst of her immense emotional and physical pain, the pastor invited the Holy Spirit to reveal truth to her in the midst of her fear and panic. Suddenly everything changed. The pastor watched as a calming wave of peace washed over her. Shari immediately stopped expressing pain; her breathing relaxed, and her countenance changed from one of panic and anguish to one of complete peace and calm. She looked at the pastor with a smile of relief and sighed, "It's finally over. I now know that I am not there anymore. Jesus said I was not bad or shameful. It wasn't my fault. Jesus said that He has removed that pain forever." She then cried tears of relief and joy, and so did the pastor. He had never seen anyone move from such pain into such genuine peace. He later told the pastor friend who had introduced him to this ministry that, "It was like I was standing on holy ground. It was indeed a very holy moment. God was in that place!"

Shari's story has been and is being replayed hundreds of thousands of times around the world as pastors, counselors, professionals, and lay ministers are administering a simple yet powerful ministry tool developed in the early 1990s called Theophostic Ministry.

What Is Theophostic Ministry?

I coined the word *theophostic* from two New Testament Greek words *Theos* (God) and *Phos* (light). These two words describe God's illuminating a previously darkened area of one's mind and thoughts. Theophostic Ministry is God's true Light, the Spirit of Christ bringing divine truth experientially into one's historical life experiences. The Spirit of Christ accomplishes this healing work, for Jesus Himself said, *"Apart from Me you can do nothing"* (Jn 15:5, italics mine). Some people have confused the name Theophostic with some other groups using the Greek word for God (*theos*) that are not Christian based and are, in fact, New Age.

Theophostic Ministry is a process in which the Holy Spirit reveals specific and personalized truth to the wounded mind of the one seeking freedom. I believe that unless the Spirit of Jesus chooses to act and heal, nothing significant can or will happen in a ministry session. In its simplest description, Theophostic Ministry is merely the minister moving aside and allowing the Spirit of Christ to expose darkness with light. It is Jesus revealing truth, freeing an individual of the lies that dominate his or her thinking, emotions, and behavior. The Spirit of Christ sets people free from lifelong fears, shame, false guilt, and anxiety, lifting the dark clouds of all emotional pain in a divinely directed moment. This is basically Romans 12:2, "Be transformed [changed] by the renewing of your mind."

Theophostic Ministry focuses on the source and origin of our pain, not on the emotional symptoms or the consequential behaviors of our lie-based pain. During the ministry session, the Theophostic counselors don't give advice, quote Scripture, or tell the person in pain the truth, since this rarely has much impact. Instead, the minister allows the Holy Spirit to reveal His specific and personalized truth to the person in pain, because that's what the wounded person needs—a healing word from God.

I spent many years seeking to help people with emotional pain by giving them my truth. I prayed with them, quoted Scripture to them, counseled them, encouraged them, and yet they still remained in pain. It wasn't until I admitted my inadequacy and depended on Christ alone to free people that I began to see consistent miracles occur.

Theophostic Ministry is having a significant impact on the

Christian counseling community worldwide. It is creating controversy for some who are accustomed to more cognitive and directive approaches while bringing freedom for many who have carried lifelong emotional pain. It has become the buzzword in Christian counseling circles, while presenting a threat to some who are entrenched in cognitive approaches. For the most part, however, it has been a breath of fresh air for those who are ministering to the emotionally wounded and downtrodden. It is often described as a "ministry tool that works."

Please hear me clearly in what I am about to say. *I am not* saying that without Theophostic Ministry people cannot find freedom, be healed of their lies, or walk in true victory. God uses many different forms of ministry to accomplish His work in His Church; Theophostic Ministry is but one of many. However, I am saying that apart from the Spirit of Christ accomplishing His experiential work in me, no effort, work, or discipline on my part will ever accomplish the renewing and spiritual maturing that God intends. Christian growth and maturity is not a "you and me, God" endeavor but my being submitted to a "work of God in me." Performance-based spiritual behavior is not spiritual maturity.

Theophostic Ministry is simply a systematized model or avenue by which we can move to a place where God can accomplish what only He can accomplish. We must never lose sight of the reality that "it is God who is at work in you, both to will and to work for His good pleasure" (Phil 2:13).

How Theophostic Ministry Began

Before I learned about Theophostic Ministry, I was surrounded by deeply wounded people needing ministry, while I, myself, was becoming defeated and burned out. I would come home each day wasted, without a drop of energy to give to my family. I was meeting with a group of incest victims and knew that the pain they carried was coming from their beliefs or interpretations of the abuse and not the abuse itself. I knew that their abuse was over and not the cause of their present emotional pain. I had tried every means possible to get them to embrace the truth, but to no avail.

I can remember having them revisit their traumatic memories over and over, but nothing happened. I watched them abreact[1] in deep emotional and physical pain as they experienced their memories, only to have the pain remain. During this abreaction I tried to give them the truth, but they could not embrace it. I would have them tell me the truth (It wasn't their fault; they were safe now; they were not dirty, shamed, defiled) and acknowledge it themselves out loud, yet they could not make it their own.

For example, if a woman was seeing herself being brutally raped in her memory, I might ask her, "Where are you right now?" Shaking and trembling, she would tell me the truth, "I am in your office."

I would continue, "Are you being raped?"

She would answer, "No, I am safe now."

I would ask, "Can he hurt you now?"

She would respond, "No, I can stop him now. He cannot ever hurt me again!"

I would ask, "How do you feel, now that you know these truths?"

She would respond, "I feel afraid."

I would ask, "Why?"

She would say, "Because he's hurting me and I'm going to die!" These irrational, illogical responses perplexed me. This woman knew the truth and could verbalize it, yet her *lie-based* thinking would override it all and she would be overwhelmed by terror.

Week after week, hour after hour, I labored with these women, until I came to the end of my self. I was driving home one evening after a group session, tired and very disappointed about what had occurred in the session (which was nothing but more of the same). I remember feeling myself give up and let go of the battle. I cried out in my spirit to God, "I can't do this anymore!"

It actually felt good to let go of the task of helping these women. I began to make plans for what I would do with the rest of my life. My wife, Sharon, and I had already developed a very successful marriage encounter weekend that we were offering to churches across the country. My initial impulse was to pour myself into this effort and gradually end my counseling relationships.

In this place of having "given up," the Lord was finally able to get through to me. As I studied the Scriptures during my prayer times, I began to understand things that I had not seen before. I am not saying that I had a divine revelation, *because I did not.* I simply began to understand Scripture where I had not before. The main truth that I had overlooked in all my years of ministry was so basic and simple that I am ashamed to admit that I had missed it. I actually gave verbal assent to it, but I didn't live it out with my life. The basic truth that I was missing was simply allowing the Spirit of Christ to be present in my ministry sessions. I always prayed both before and after our sessions. However, I never actually invited the Holy Spirit to participate, and never expected Him to address the victims in their traumatic pain. Here I was, a Christian counselor and minister, and yet I had forgotten about Jesus. What I had done in my counseling practice was the same thing that I had done in the church ministries I had served in earlier years. I had learned to "work the programs," to grow the church in attendance, to keep people coming and keep those in attendance happy, all the while rarely experiencing the presence of Christ.

When people experience the presence of Christ, there is *always* miraculous change. I am afraid that much of what we call spiritual encounters with God are program-driven events, orchestrated and manipulated to create a pleasurable moment for the recipient. Yet, if what we have experienced has not transformed our lives at some level, then it is questionable as to whether we have had a genuine God experience. The emotional response we have during the event is not a determining factor of the validity of the experience. We can have a warm emotional and nostalgic experience at a James Taylor concert. However, this cannot be said to be a spiritual moment. (Sorry, baby boomers, this does not qualify as a God experience.) However, each of us can know God experientially in those places where we have buried and carried pain and woundedness, if we are willing to go there, face our pain, and receive from Him.

Everyone Needs True Healing

Most people have not suffered a severe trauma, but everyone has been wounded at some level—all of us have memories that are imbedded with lies. We all need our minds renewed. When we experientially "know" God in these places and receive His truth, we will find His rest, joy, and peace. Paul said, "I pray that the *eyes of your heart* may be enlightened, so that you may *know* what is the hope of His calling, what are the riches of the glory of His inheritance in the saints" (Eph 1:18, italics mine). As the "eyes of our heart" are opened we will see who we are in Christ and come to "know" the love of Christ experientially.

This is my prayer for you as you read this book. You can find freedom from the lies you believe and walk in His peace. You can be free, totally free in each lie-based memory, and never have to worry about bondage again.

Just ask Andrew.

Andrew told me that even though he had abstained from homosexual practices for the eight years he had been a Christian, he felt tempted with strong urges every day. Still, he felt that he was victorious because he had not succumbed to any homosexual behavior. Andrew held the mistaken belief that abstinence means victory. This is not victory. Victory occurs only when the battle and struggle are over—for good. Andrew was not free of the battle.

Andrew and I spent about four hours going through the many childhood traumas and events that had led to his sexual disorientation. By the conclusion of the process, the Lord Jesus had set him free from any homosexual desires. Months later he wrote me: "I have not had one homosexual urge in over three months and I have *not* had to work at it! Before this freedom, I could not go an hour!" Andrew's thinking had changed. His freedom was real. Now he could rest. He had experienced true emotional, spiritual, and physical release.

You can, too.

Special note to pastors and counselors:
Please understand that this book is *not* training in how to do Theophostic Ministry. *Please do not* attempt to administer this process on others without having completed the full basic training. Many of the primary principles of administering Theophostic Ministry are not included in this book, and you may experience negative results if you attempt this process without adequate training. This book does *not* contain all you need to administer the process. ***You may cause more harm than good if you seek to lead a person to the places of pain in his or her mind without all the tools you need to deal with what you open up.*** Please be wise as you minister to hurting people.

Warning: Some of you reading this book may become uncomfortable with a few of the stories that I share. The content of the stories may very well trigger the pain in your own past. If you become bothered by a story, I would suggest that you skip over it until you can be in a place where you can receive qualified ministry and care.

ONE

The Pain Is Gone—ALL Gone!

Margaret's Story

Margaret was clearly in intense emotional pain. As she sat in the chair in front of me in my office, she resisted eye contact by either looking away or holding her head down in a shamed posture. Each time I spoke to her, her answers were short and truncated. When I asked her a question, she would hesitate and then respond as if I had called her back from some distant place in her mind. When she answered, her inner pain would become more acute and apparent, as though my questions were forcing her to connect with a painful reality that she wanted to avoid. Her eyes filled with tears and she held tightly to her frayed and wadded tissue, nervously twisting and folding it over and over.

Desperate for freedom from her inner turmoil, Margaret had traveled over a thousand miles to see me because previous attempts at counseling hadn't proven effective. When Margaret was eight years old, her father had begun to sexually and physically abuse her, and he had continued to do so throughout her childhood. Her adult life had been filled with depression and defeat, failed marriages, joblessness, and distrust of others. Her doctor had prescribed heavy doses of medication.

In the past I would have told Margaret that she would need to see me for two to five years of counseling, and even then the best she could hope for was to become more functional and live a more productive life. Even after years and years of counseling, the incest survivors with whom I had worked still had some residual pain in their memories and all had some difficulty being sexually intimate with their spouses. Sexual intimacy was a guaranteed "trigger" that would incite their emotional pain from the sexual abuse.

Yet today it would be different. She would not be coming back for weekly sessions or joining a survivor's recovery group; today she would find freedom from the pain in her abuse memories.

I began by asking her if she truly wanted to be free of her pain, and she told me yes. I then shared the Theophostic Ministry principles and asked her if she wanted to undergo Theophostic Ministry, and she said yes. I asked her to focus on the emotional pain she was feeling and to follow this emotional "smoke trail" back to the memories that were the source of that pain. The goal of our session would be to receive a decisive word from the Holy Spirit, which would, in turn, release her from the pain of the lies that were the true source of her emotional discomfort.

Before we began the session, Margaret's traumatic memories had shamed her, condemned her, and made her feel dirty, nasty, and somehow responsible. Yet as she processed her traumatic memories, one by one, her emotional pain disappeared as the Spirit of Jesus revealed His truth to her. At the end of the session, I asked Margaret to bring back to mind all the memories of her father molesting her, and asked her to tell me what she felt. She exclaimed, "It's gone! All the shame, guilt, and pain are gone!"

To this day, Margaret reports complete release from the

pain and shame she had felt in her abuse memories. Margaret is free.[1]

Paula's Story

Paula was over seventy years old when she came to me for help shortly after one of her relatives had died. She told me that as she had been standing next to the coffin, she had noticed that all the other family members were expressing genuine grief over the man's death. Many had been crying and were overwhelmed with sadness, but all she had felt were rage and a sense of relief that he was dead. The longer she had remained at the graveside, the more her anger had swelled. Finally she had excused herself and gone home.

This experience had confused Paula, and she had come to me for Theophostic Ministry. She had tried to understand her feelings, but nothing in her conscious mind explained her anger and rage.

During the Theophostic session an old, "forgotten" event emerged. When Paula was only eleven years old, the man who had recently died, who was a distant relative, had snuck into her room one night and forcefully raped her. The pain had been excruciating, and the fear and confusion overwhelming. After the attack, she had quietly cried in the bathroom while she had washed the blood out of her underclothing. She had decided to keep quiet because she felt no one would believe her, since this person was favored and respected in the family. She had also felt a great sense of dirtiness and believed that she had been defiled by what he had done.

Paula buried the memory, but her rage and shame haunted

her throughout her life. Her disruptive anger had filled her relationships with turmoil, and she had suffered from addictions, compulsions, and four broken marriages. Her anger had finally made its grand entrance at her abuser's graveside. Yet after several sessions of Theophostic Ministry, Paula's rage was gone and her mind was at peace. This one repressed event had robbed her of joy for over sixty years, but it is never too late to find freedom from our pain.

June's Story

June came to me suffering from what she described as an irrational fear. I explained to her that there is no such thing as irrational fear, despite what others may teach. Fear is the natural response to a perceived danger, threat, or harm. When we experience feelings of fear for no apparent reason, this is not irrational; it's simply irrational in the present context. When something triggers a lie-based memory, we feel the *rational* fear, shame, and guilt of the original event.

June argued that her fear made no sense, saying that for the last six months it had come each night shortly after she went to bed and everything was quiet. She knew she was safe, and couldn't understand why she felt so afraid. I asked her if she had ever felt this same fear in other situations. She said that she had, but it had been under different circumstances and never at night in her bed.

We tried to find the source of her fear but did not get very far in her first Theophostic session. However, we were able to reach several memories that held negative emotions, and freedom came to those places. Yet June's fear remained. I asked her to go home and at bedtime to be aware of what her mind focused upon just before the fear surfaced. The next week she reported what she thought was a strange discovery—the fear was somehow connected to her clock ticking. She also realized that her bedtime fears had begun after she had purchased this clock. Her solution was to get rid of the clock and thereby be rid of the fears.

I realized that the clock was not the problem, and that the ticking had triggered the lie-based pain of a painful memory. I asked her to think about lying in her bed, listening to the ticking of the clock, and to allow the fear to surface. Within a few moments she felt the fear. I applied the Theophostic principles, and within a few moments she found herself in a frightening memory from her childhood. One night someone had come into her room, molested her, and threatened to kill her if she screamed or made any noise. While the trauma was happening she had dissociated by focusing on the ticking of a grandfather clock that was in her room.

Her newly purchased clock had become a nightly trigger that surfaced the fear and pain contained in the memory of that childhood experience. As June was willing to go through the memory, feel the fear, and identify what she had believed about the abuse, we invited the Holy Spirit to reveal His truth to her. As she received His truth, the fear vanished and His perfect peace took its place. Later she reported that the clock no longer triggered any fear, and she was having peaceful and restful sleep. She had also decided to keep the clock as a reminder of God's healing.

Sandra's Story

Sandra had been in and out of mental hospitals and was heavily medicated. Overall, she was an emotional wreck. She could not work and lived with her parents even though she was thirty years old. Her misinformed yet well-meaning pastor had warned her to stay away from Theophostic Ministry. He had read some of the misinformation being propagated on the Internet. (It is incredible how God takes that which is designed to discredit this ministry and uses it to bring about good.) Out of curiosity, she had looked up the word theophostic on the Internet and had found our web page (www.theophostic.com). What she read on the web page was contrary to what her pastor had told her. As she read the testimonies of others who had reported healing from their lifelong emotional struggles, she felt hopeful for her own situation.

When Sandra came to my office she was as emotionally downtrodden as any person I had ever seen. She handed me a stack of medical records that documented her journey over the last fifteen years. She had already spent over $50,000 out of her own pocket over the many years of treatment, yet she was still in great distress. Her extensive medical records, from a host of counselors and doctors, revealed a list of diagnoses that included bipolar disorder, chronic depression, border-line personality disorder, dissociation, obsessive-compulsive disorder, panic disorder, and several other phobias. She sat quietly and nonresponsively as I skimmed through her file.

When I finished I laid it on the table beside me and asked her to look up at me. Her eyes were lightless and filled with despair. I looked into her eyes and asked her what I ask everyone who comes to see me: "Sandra, do you want to be free of your pain? Do you want Jesus to release you?" I needed to know what her will was in the moment. Not everyone that comes for help wants to be free. She slowly but clearly responded, "Yes."

I said, "If this is true, then you meet all biblical requirements—faith and willful submission to Him—as far as I can tell, for God to release you of your pain." I went on to ask her, "Are you willing to go to the memories that hold the source of your pain? And are you willing to feel all of the pain and identify the true reason for why you feel the way you do?" There was a longer pause before she responded, but eventually she spoke with a clear and firm "yes."

Sandra had scheduled several sessions with me, which is what I recommend for those who are highly traumatized by numerous painful memories. Day by day, we visited memory after memory, for hours on end, walking through some of the most horrific experiences that can be imagined. The presence of Christ came into each and every memory, in the midst of seemingly endless pain, bringing perfect peace with His truth. At the end of the three days, Sandra said that she felt peace and genuine release.

Sandra came to see me over four years ago. She is no longer depressed, she is no longer dissociated (she has completely integrated), and she is no longer obsessed or compulsive. I still see Sandra from time to time, because we live in the same town. When she experiences pain because of additional lie-based memories, she comes to see me in order to bring Christ's healing to those memories as well. Mind renewal is a lifelong journey as God continually exposes our lie-based thinking so He might release us with His truth.

Margaret's, Paula's, June's, and Sandra's stories are typical of those who receive Theophostic Ministry. The healing experienced is genuine and lasting. I receive literally thousands of emails, cards, and letters from people all around the world who are using this approach to ministry and are giving witness of the glorious things that God is doing in the lives of wounded people.

Part of My Story

A few years ago, I was listening to a speaker making a presentation. I had thought that I was going to be asked to present, but at the last minute the schedule had been changed and I had been eliminated. As I sat there listening, I noticed a growing anxiety and a tightness in my chest. In the past I would have dismissed this and suppressed the feelings, often covering them over with anger or feelings of offense. I have learned that many negative emotions, such as fear, helplessness, anxiety, and worry are often hidden by anger. I got up from my seat and went into a small back room. As I sat in the chair, I allowed myself to feel the increasing anxiety. I began to apply the Theophostic steps and soon discovered the memory in which I had first felt that same emotion.

I remembered a time from the second or third grade when I was on the playground. Two children had been appointed to choose sides for the game we were about to play. I was the very last child to be chosen for a team. I watched as the two team captains argued over who had to have me on their team. I felt rejected, unloved, not good enough, and angry. The messages underneath these feelings were lies that I believed, and were the source of the pain I was experiencing. I continued with the Theophostic process, and soon the Spirit of Christ revealed these words to my heart and mind: "I love and want you and I chose you." The instant I understood these words, the anxiety and tightness in my chest vanished. I went back into the conference and listened to the rest of the lecture.

My memory of what happened on the playground is not very traumatic, yet it contained lies that were hindering my adult life. I share this personal experience to say that healing is for everyone, not just those who have been traumatized with abuse. When I feel bad feelings, I am prone to make poor decisions and act out my pain. However, the more I find freedom and am released to walk in God's perfect peace, the more good choices I can freely make.

Every person on the face of this earth is carrying some level of pain. We have all been infested with lie-based thinking. If you think you have not been infected, just ask those who know you. If you become aware of how you are feeling throughout the day, you will begin to pick up on when your lies are being triggered. For example, when that fellow gets your parking place at the shopping center, be aware of what you are feeling. The emotion you feel is likely based in a memory of another time when you felt something similar. Most of us have opportunities for healing every day, if we will just watch, feel, and listen. I know I do.

If you are hurting or know others who are, Theophostic Ministry may be the very thing for which you have been searching. Life doesn't have to be an emotional struggle. You don't have to settle for tolerable recovery or wait years for healing of your lie-based pain. You can experience genuine recovery now. As you read this book, I hope that you will be sensitive to areas of your life in which you need healing. God desires this for you. He desires that you walk in truth and come to know Him experientially.

THE BASIC PRINCIPLES OF
THEOPHOSTIC MINISTRY

This is a very abbreviated discussion of some of the basic principles of Theophostic Ministry. For a complete understanding of this ministry approach you will want to order the complete training program. (See ordering information at the end of this book or visit www.theophostic.com.)

Principle One: *My present emotional pain is rarely caused by my present situation.*
More often than not, the present emotional trouble is the symptom of a deeper wound where lie-based thinking was originally implanted.

Principle Two: *Everything we know, feel, or are mentally aware of has its roots in a first-time experience.*
When we react negatively to a present situation, our negative feelings come from what we believe in memories of original experiences that are similar to the present situation. This is an automatic emotional response that has great bearing on what behaviors we choose to act out. We tend to act out the way we feel.

Principle Three: *If we try to resolve our present pain and conflict without resolving our historical lie-based woundedness, we will at best find only temporary relief. However, if we find healing for our past, we can redeem our present.*

Counseling and ministry typically focus on trying to change the present behavior of a person. This is only a stopgap and will not result in true victory if the underlying lies are not addressed. This also fosters performance-based spirituality, which is rooted in works salvation.

Principle Four: *The negative emotion we currently feel is an "echo" of the past, providing an opportunity and an open window for the exposure of the lies in the wounds of our lives.*
If we choose to follow the emotional "smoke trail" back to its memory origin, we can discover the initial lie-based belief that is causing the emotional pain. Here we can find complete freedom as we receive truth from the Spirit of Christ.

Principle Five: *For emotional healing, we need to identify three basic elements: the present emotional pain, the original memory container, and the original lie(s).*
Emotional pain is what we feel in our present state or is that which surfaces when a memory-based lie is triggered. The memory container is the original experience where the lie-based pain was implanted. The original lie is the belief that was implanted in the original memory that is causing the present pain.

Principle Six: *If we believe a lie, it may as well be the truth, because the consequences will be much the same.*
If we believe a lie to be the truth, then it will play itself out as though it were true. Yet when the Spirit of Christ

brings truth into our memory, He replaces the lie with truth, and we will find genuine release and peace.

Principle Seven: *To be free of the lies we believe, we must first identify and embrace them rather than suppress, deny, or denounce them.*

It is a natural inclination to deny the lies we believe and to bury our pain. Yet doing this maintains a perpetual cycle of defeat in our lives. As long as the lies remain embedded in the memory, they will cause pain every time they are triggered by similar life situations.

Principle Eight: *In order to be free we must come to realize how utterly bound we are to the lie and how helpless we are, apart from the Spirit of Christ setting us free, in overcoming its debilitating grip on our lives.*

This is the same place people were in the New Testament when Christ healed them. In our despair, the power of God is made known. The apostle Paul declared, "My grace is sufficient for you, for power is perfected in weakness. Most gladly, therefore, I will rather boast about my weaknesses, that the power of Christ may dwell in me" (2 Cor 12:9).

Principle Nine: *Neither we nor anyone else can talk us out of the lies we believe. We will be free only when we receive the truth from the One who is Truth.*

God is not limited to any means of delivering this truth to us. (Theophostic Ministry is but one avenue He can use to do this.) However, much of the counseling going on today, and many of the training seminars and self-help books being written, are based on the belief that, "If a person can be led to see what is wrong in his or her thinking and then be provided with truth, this person can choose to replace his or her false thinking with the truth and then be different." This has had limited success, at best, and mainly with those with the most self-discipline and determination. Cognitively receiving truth will have very little or no impact on releasing a person from the pain in his or her life apart from the intervention of the Holy Spirit, who leads us into all truth. The false assumption is that people can walk in victory simply by choosing to think differently. This is simply positive thinking and self-effort, which are at the heart of works salvation. The truth is, most people already logically know why they are in pain, and logically hold the truths they need, but still are in emotional misery and still cannot find their way to freedom.

Principle Ten: *When we know the truth experientially (when we receive truth from God in our memory experience) we can walk in genuine maintenance-free victory in these areas of our life.*

When the lies in our memories are replaced with truth, they no longer have power to create pain. Since our emotional pain often motivates our inappropriate behavior, we will be able to walk in true victory in these specific areas when the lie is no longer present.

Principle Eleven: *In times of crisis or in emotionally charged situations, our experiential knowledge (the beliefs we hold that we have learned through experience) overrides our logical truth (cognitive truth such as memorized Scripture verses).*

It is difficult to appropriate biblical truth when what we have learned experientially is contrary to this logically held truth. Yet as we let go of the lie-based sources and take hold of the truth that God has for us experientially, our minds easily appropriate truth we have known only cognitively before. When we experientially hear God say, "I love you" within our painful memory experiences, we find it easy to believe that we are loved by God and fully accepted by Him.

Principle Twelve: *If a person sins he will experience emotional pain in his life at some point.*

For example, if a Christian commits the sin of adultery, he or she will experience emotional pain from lost relationship, lost reputation, and genuine shame and guilt. Sin-based pain can be removed only through confession and appropriating the atoning work of Christ on the cross. The only cure for sin is the cross. This pain is different from the pain one carries as a consequence of lie-based thinking. Lie-based pain can be removed only as the lies that are causing the pain are replaced with truth.

TWO

Genuine Recovery Versus Tolerable Recovery

What Is Tolerable Recovery?

I was raised Southern Baptist and served in their churches for over seventeen years before beginning a counseling ministry in 1991. After years of working with adult incest victims and seeing only marginal progress and recovery, I was burning out. I believed that the best any person in emotional pain could hope for was to "get better," and that healing from the deep wounds caused by things such as rape, incest, or ritual abuse would take years and years. I honestly did not think complete resolution from severe trauma was possible. It seemed more reasonable to teach people how to compensate and live life in spite of one's losses.

My approach to helping people was similar to most traditional Christian counseling practices. I sought to understand why a person was in trouble, conflict, or pain, and looked for ways that the Bible could be applied to his or her particular situation. I saw myself as a trouble-shooter of human issues and a biblical applicator to these troubled places. I believed that people were in pain, conflict, or trouble because they either had sinned or believed lies, which produced a predictable emotional upheaval from which they would make their choices, resulting in more problems and more emotional pain. I believed that their only way of escape was to know and act on truth.

Most counselors agree that recovery is defined as moving a person emotionally, mentally, physically, and spiritually from an assumed undesirable place (addiction, obsession, depression, anger) to an assumed *better place* (happy, healthy, spiritually and mentally free). Someone in "recovery" might say, "I am not quite there yet, but I am closer than I was. I am not drinking, smoking, raging, or as depressed, compulsive, obsessed, controlled, or controlling as I was, because I have learned to manage it thus far."

For most people, getting better is not such a bad place to be. For example, the medicated bipolar is more happy being chemically stabilized after years of highs and lows. Emotional stability is a welcome improvement. Feeling better is an improvement. I call this *tolerable recovery,* which is not what Jesus offered people.[1]

Don't Be Deceived

Many ministers and counselors are successful in discerning the core beliefs that cause a person pain. The problem is not in discovering the reason for one's pain, but in knowing what to do when it is discovered. Traditional counseling tends to focus on helping people by supplying them with new knowledge, developing new habits and skills, developing better methods of communication, overcoming bad habits through support, and maintaining some level of abstinence.

Those who believe that they can allow people to walk in freedom simply by supplying them with biblical truth gravely misunderstand what the Bible teaches and overestimate the power of self-determination and human willpower. We cannot keep the Law or apply truth through self-effort. Scripture teaches just the opposite. The Bible says, "When the commandment came, sin became alive and I died" (Rom 7:9). The Law was given to expose us, not to heal us. Yet, we often equate knowledge, controlled behavior, willpower, and self-effort with spiritual maturity.

I know, because that was exactly my approach to counseling. I believed that all I could do was offer truth and then trust that the person had enough willpower and determination to apply that truth. This was nothing more than legalism and works salvation, and it is an approach that produces only more frustration, hopelessness, and defeat. Only those people with strong self-discipline and determination can have any measure of "success." As I just said, the Law of God was not given to save us but rather to expose us and condemn us and to become a "tutor" that would drive us to the mercy and grace of God found in Christ.

Jesus didn't offer people tolerable recovery. When Christ healed people, the healing was always complete and total.[2] When the lame man told Him that he wanted to be healed, Jesus healed him and told him to walk (see Jn 5). He did not say, "My friend, put these braces on your legs and take My arm for support, and come hobble along with Me down to the Jerusalem Physical Therapy Center. In no time you will be walking all on your own. Now friend, you must understand, you may walk again, but you will probably have a slight limp.

You will never be able to run or dance and you may be required to wear these braces for the rest of your life. Be of good cheer, for at least you won't be sitting here on the curb, begging. You will be in better shape than you are now, and that will be tolerable. Come hobble along with Me, for you are healed ... sort of. *So take up your bed and limp!"* No, the healing that Jesus offered was complete and maintenance-free. This man did not have to work at walking, focus on his steps, or fear relapse; he was healed!

True Christian victory has nothing to do with me— it's God's grace and Christ at work in me. True victory is maintenance-free and is "easy" because it is not based on my self-effort or willpower. Jesus called us to take on His yoke that is light and easy (see Mt 11:29-30). Yet few Christians would describe their Christian walk as easy. Much of what they believe doctrinally and theologically is never realized experientially. This doesn't have to be!

More biblical truth and personal application of that truth will not result in true freedom, which is effortless. It may give us all the "right" answers, yet we will continue to suffer. We are good at saying the words, such as "My God shall supply all your needs"(Phil 4:19), "I can do all things through Christ"(Phil 4:13, KJV), or "We are more than conquerors"(Rom 8:37, KJV), and yet struggling to find entry into their reality. Just because we believe these statements logically does not mean that we know them experientially.

Beyond Truth to Experience

Freedom—*genuine recovery*—comes from going beyond knowledge into experience. We must experientially discover the truth of who we are in Christ, and thereby come to "know" the love Christ has for us. God wants us to "know the love of Christ which *surpasses knowledge,* that you may be filled up to all the fullness of God" (Eph 3:19, emphasis mine). This goes beyond a cognitive understanding.

I am *not* saying that personal Bible study and instruction aren't valuable or important. The Bible clearly states that we should "study to show [ourselves] approved" (2 Tim 2:15, KJV) and we should "let the word of Christ richly dwell within [us], with all wisdom teaching and admonishing one another with psalms and hymns and spiritual songs" (Col 3:16). However, knowledge without experience is like faith without works—it is dead (see Jas 2:17). We need to know God experientially as well as cognitively.

Many have difficulty living the Christian life, not because they lack zeal or determination to do better, but because of lies they believe. They may know the truth, but their memories are permeated with lies, and their knowledge of God is cognitive rather than experiential. Every lie we believe hinders us from living effortlessly in the finished work of Christ. When we find freedom from a lie, we can walk victoriously and effortlessly in that area of our life. The lies we believe keep us in bondage to the negative emotions and the behavior that follows.

Jerry came to me very angry with his father and ready to dissolve the family business. He said that all his life his father had been overbearing and critical and had made him feel worthless and inadequate. He said that the way he was treated caused him to feel like a helpless little boy. I told him about the principles of Theophostic Ministry and asked him if he would be willing to find his memories of where he first felt these feelings. He agreed.

Jerry had many different memories of times when his father had said or done hurtful things to him, and in each case lies were implanted into Jerry's thinking. I led him through the healing process, and Jerry reported perfect peace in all the memories we had visited.

I ran into Jerry a couple of years later and he shared with me this wonderful testimony. He said he was still in business with his father, even though his father had not changed. Then he told me, "He just cannot stir me up anymore! It's like his words have lost all power to penetrate." He went on to say that he now saw his father as a very wounded, angry, and unhappy man. He said that he hoped that someday his father would be willing to go to the places of pain where he needed to find healing. When I asked Jerry if he had to work at maintaining this newfound peace when working around his dad, he told me no. He said that it was effortless!

Like Jerry, we are hindered by the lies we believe from living effortlessly in the finished work of Christ. Every time we find freedom from a lie that has hindered us, we are able to stand victoriously in the healed area of our thinking, without any effort on our part to maintain it.

Genuine Recovery Is Maintenance-Free

Over the last six years my wife, Sharon, and I have *not* worked on our marriage, yet our marriage is stronger today simply because we have been faithful to go to our own lie-based thinking and have allowed the Spirit of Christ to give us truth. One by one, we are bringing the presence of Christ into our individual lie-based memories, and fewer and fewer things cause us pain or trigger negative feelings. I haven't arrived at total peace (all you need to do is ask Sharon about this). Yet, I'm freer today than ever before.

True victory is the absence of battle and struggle. True victory cannot be claimed unless the enemy has been defeated, the dust has settled, the victory flag has been raised, and the war is over. Victory does not require me to defend the same territory in future battles. Tolerable recovery, which includes abstinence, stands in sharp contrast to the blind man who received his sight. His response was, "one thing I do know that, whereas I was blind, *now* I see." (Jn 9:25, emphasis mine). He did not say, "Once I was blind but now I can see a little better and am seeing more and more as I continue in my recovery process, and I am really hoping that I don't go blind again anytime soon."

When Christ heals, God's Spirit replaces the lies that are causing the pain with His truth, memory by memory, lie by lie. When a counselor or minister implants truth into the wounded person's mind, the lies still linger. Cognitive truth is not enough. Truth must go down into the heart before it results in true freedom, and freedom comes from experiencing Jesus.

Let me say clearly that Theophostic Ministry will *not* result in complete recovery of *all* wounds in a single session. In later chapters you will read several stories of people who spent many hours and several sessions going through the Theophostic process in order to identify and replace the lies embedded in their memories. Freedom comes memory by memory, lie by lie. I have been actively pursuing my own mind renewal using Theophostic Ministry for over six years. As I am stirred emotionally, I follow the pain to its memory source. I am finding peace in each place I go.

Some people come to me with years of trauma-filled memories piled one on top of another. I may spend many sessions with a person who has experienced numerous traumatic events, but I also see instantaneous recovery *memory by memory* in each session. Even though it may take many sessions with some people, when a person is led to the position where he or she is ready to receive from the Lord, incredible results will occur.

When Is a Person Completely Healed?

Where is the finish line for this process? When does a person become completely whole? Mind renewal is a lifelong journey. The finish line is at one of two places: when we die or when the Lord returns. However, we can go to the places where the lies are stored and find release, lie by lie. With each lie we remove, we are better able to appropriate the deeper truths of who we are in Christ.

I am learning to be aware of my emotional pain in my daily walk. More often than not, I am choosing to allow the Holy

Spirit to lead me to the places in my mind where I am harboring lies that are causing me pain. As a result of these choices, I am becoming more and more free! I have come to the place where I have decided that I no longer want people and circumstances to dictate my emotional status. I want to be free and to learn to *be at peace in whatever circumstance I find myself* (see Phil 4:11). How about you?

THREE

The True Source of Our Emotional Pain

Looking in All the Wrong Places

When we suffer from emotional pain, we usually look in one of two places to determine the source of that pain. We either try to find someone or something in the present to blame or we look to our past and blame those who have hurt us in childhood. However, if we seek to find the cause of our pain in either of these two places, we will never find resolution and never know the peace that God has for us.

If something happens between Sharon and me that stirs up a negative emotion within me, my initial reaction is to blame her and accuse her of being the cause of my pain. I might tell her, "You make me so mad!" or "I wouldn't feel this way if you would just stop _____."[1] If it were indeed true that my wife was the cause of my pain, then I could never be free of that pain unless she changed. When we blame another person for our painful feelings, we are giving that person power over our emotions. This doesn't have to be.

Of course, there are times when a person in the present is the original source of our hurt. For instance, if you discover that your spouse has been unfaithful, then much of the pain you feel can be directly attributed to his or her actions.

However, similar forms of betrayal that you may have experienced in the past will also surface along with the pain you feel from the present betrayal. If you were abandoned or betrayed as a child, then the pain you experienced at that time will flood the current situation and create an "emotional overload."

Emotional overload occurs when a painful situation in the present is inundated with "old" pain, causing the current situation to feel more painful than it should. When we experience emotional overload, our emotional response will be more intense than the situation may warrant. For example, if a person takes our parking place, our emotional response might call for some mild irritation but not rage. The rage is coming from somewhere else.

Not only do we blame people in our present life for our emotional pain, we also blame painful childhood experiences. While this might seem logical, especially considering all the horrible things that some people have endured in their childhood, past events are not the present source of our pain. While it's true that had an incest victim been raised in a happy, loving, and caring family, he or she would be in a different emotional place today, nevertheless, the abuse and mistreatment that person received in childhood are not the source of his or her emotional pain today.

Granted, the initial abuse did cause a traumatic reaction and may have been physically and emotionally overwhelming, but the event itself is not the *present* source of the person's emotional state. If it were, then abuse victims could never find peace because they could never undo what had been done to them in the past. They would always be victims of abuse, no matter how long they lived or how much ministry or counseling they received. The original trauma may have been physically painful, but the body has healed. Original trauma doesn't cause lingering emotional pain. Rather, *the source of our present pain is found in the interpretation we have given the event.*

If we find ourselves blaming people in our present life or those who have hurt us in childhood, we will be perpetually wounded. However, Theophostic Ministry seeks to discover what we believe, and looks to the Spirit of Christ for freeing truth. Freedom results, not from blaming others or by undoing our past (which is impossible), but from identifying the lies attached to our life events and then receiving truth from the presence of Christ.

The Role of Memories and Pain

The memory is the mind's container of historical data and interpretive information. If the memory holds information that is true, it cannot be changed. So, if it's true that little Mary's grandfather raped her and that she was mistreated at school, abandoned by her mother, and raised by an occult group in the deserts of Nevada, these facts will remain in her memory. Facts can't be changed, nor are they the cause of present emotional pain.

Little Mary's beliefs about the abuse—not the abuse itself— are the cause of her pain. If she believes that she caused the abuse, then she will feel guilt. If she believes that the rape defiled her, she will feel dirty and shameful. If she believes that her mother abandoned her because there was something wrong with her, then she will feel inadequate, worthless, and unlovable. If she believes that she belongs to the occult, she will feel trapped, helpless, and powerless. Mary's beliefs about the abuse are the source of her emotional pain.

Whenever something painful happens to a child, the child will interpret that event and store the interpretation in the memory of the event. Even when the child becomes an adult, his or her interpretation of the painful event becomes the source of his or her present pain every time something or someone triggers the memory. For example, Carol was abducted and raped by a man in her neighborhood when she was fourteen years old. Now thirty-six years old and married, she still has panic attacks when her spouse tries to be intimate with her. When her husband goes on a business trip she becomes so fearful that she calls him several times a day.

This happens because God created her mind to work by way of association. Earlier I said that our minds record both the information of the events and our interpretation of the events. That means that every experience we had as children has been stored in our experiential memory bank, along with our emotional responses to and interpretation of the event. Any time someone says or does something, or any time something happens that consciously or subconsciously reminds us of a similar situation in our past, our mind brings this information to the forefront and we feel what we felt the first time it happened.

Repressed memories are as powerful and dictating as conscious memories; it doesn't matter that we aren't conscious of them. Every time anything occurs that is even remotely similar to the original event—even a word or a look—the original lie and emotions will emerge, causing discomfort. When we experience an event, our brains not only record the facts of the situation, such as who, what, when, and where, but they also record insignificant elements, such as the color of the person's clothing, someone snoring in the next room, or the toy bear on the dresser across the room. Any of this recorded information holds the potential to trigger the emotional pain we felt during the event.

For example, if during a childhood trauma I fixated on a teddy bear in my room, later when I see a teddy bear in a store it might trigger intense feelings of anxiety. Or if my boss asks me how the report I am working on is coming along, my response will depend on the beliefs I have stored in my experiential data. I may feel inadequate and shamed or feel just the opposite, depending on my history. If I interpreted the original event through lies, then my thinking will be lie-based, and similar events will trigger those same lies.

What Is Lie-Based Thinking?

To understand how Theophostic Ministry works, you need to understand the concept I have already referred to as *lie-based thinking*. The mind contains information that is a composite of lies and truth. Logically, we know the difference. I know there is no Santa Claus, even though as a child I believed there was. I know that two plus two is four and that Canada is somewhere north of Kentucky. This is what I call logical truth. My logical mind also contains information such as "My God shall supply all your needs" (Phil 4:19), "The Lord is my strength and my shield" (Ps 28:7), and "I can do all things through Christ"

(Phil 4:13, KJV). I can spout off these verses with ease and impress my Sunday school class with the "right" answer. Yet, while I know these things to be true on a cognitive level, I may not know it on an experiential level.

Unfortunately, even though we may know the correct answer in a given situation, many of our choices and responses are based on what we believe experientially. If we truly believe that God is our shield and protector, then we should never live in fear. If we believe that God is the supplier of all our needs, then we should never be anxious over finances. If we believe that God is in control of our lives, then we should never worry about what is happening around us. Yet what we feel reveals the truth about what we truly believe. Our emotions expose our core beliefs.

I do not think it is possible to change our core experiential beliefs through willpower or by simply telling ourselves the truth. Many people have tried memorizing Scripture, posting positive statements on their mirrors and refrigerators, and thinking positive thoughts (which are all good things in and of themselves) and yet still walk around in emotional defeat. We feel what we believe experientially—not logically. As much as we would like to believe otherwise, our emotions will always expose what we truly believe. *If what we believe is false, then it is lie-based thinking.*

The Power of Lie-Based Thinking

What we think controls how we feel. If we believe a lie is true, then it doesn't matter that it's not, for it will have the same consequences on our lives. If we believe we are shameful because we were sexually violated as children, it does not matter that we were innocent. The shaming lie will work itself out in our lives as though it were true, and the consequences will be the same. Here are some additional examples of this:

- One day I was working in our backyard on a project. It was hot and I was tired. My lovely wife came outside to check on me out of kindness and concern. She walked over to where I was working and asked, "Why did you do that like that?" My immediate response was anger—*I do not need her out here criticizing my work!*—and I said, "Why don't you and your criticism go back in the house and leave me alone!" Suddenly the forty-five-year-old man became a hurting little eight-year-old who was feeling like he could not do anything right.

- Years ago, I was serving a church in Kansas City, Missouri, as a minister to single adults. There was a woman who worked as a secretary in the church office who was deathly afraid of spiders. I knew this and teased her from time to time about it. One time I put a big black rubber spider in her top desk drawer as a joke. As it turned out, it wasn't very funny. She found the spider but nearly had heart failure. I felt bad for playing such a cruel trick, but she had no real reason to be afraid. The spider was not a spider at all, yet she believed it was real and because of this she felt real fear and panic ... for a piece of molded rubber.

Much of this experiential knowing is not always consciously present. What we are thinking at the conscious level is often contrary to what we are thinking and believing at the subconscious, experiential level. When a person suffering from claustrophobia walks into an elevator and begins to panic, she is not consciously thinking about the time her mother locked her in the closet all day. Instead, she feels the suffocation experienced in the original event as though it were still happening.[2] This repressed memory contains the source of her panic, but she can give no logical explanation for her present feelings.

Lie-Based Solutions for Pain

Most people are surprised to discover how much their lives are dictated by the lies they believe that were implanted during difficult moments in their childhood. For example, infidelity usually has little to do with the marriage itself. More often than not, the motivation for an affair is rooted in a desire to resolve emotional pain that comes from lie-based thinking.

Before Theophostic Ministry's inception, I counseled Christian people's infidelity *solely* as a sin problem, as a willful choice of immorality. While adultery is a sin, the feelings driving the decision to commit adultery are usually rooted in a person's lie-based thinking. It and other sinful behaviors are often predictable consequences of deception, producing emotional pain that consummates in sinful choices. James 1:14-15 says, "Each one is tempted when he is carried away and enticed by his own lust. Then when lust has conceived, it gives birth to sin; and when sin is accomplished, it brings forth death." Notice the stages one passes through before a sin is committed. First there is temptation or lie-based deception (you can be tempted only by that which you believe you need or want). Then you are "carried away by your own lust." In the original language the word translated here as *lust* does not suggest sexual feelings, but rather any strong passion, desire, or emotion. When someone triggers my lie-based thinking, my lust or strong emotion is stirred. When I embrace this strong passion, it gives birth to sinful behavior.

Can you see the problem with making sin the focal point in a counseling or ministry session? If I make sin the primary focus and do not address the lie-based thinking, I will be forcing the person to enter into a defeat-confess-repent-adjust-perform cycle.[3]

Sex is rarely the motivation for people engaging in an affair. While it's usually a consequence of the relationship, it is rarely the driving force behind it. People tend to commit adultery because emotional pain has surfaced in their present relationship and they believe that the adulterous relationship promises some level of relief. When their strong painful emotions are stirred up, they deceptively see the other relationship as a solution to their present emotional pain. Christians and non-Christians alike are often driven by their lie-based pain. The only difference is, the Christian must violate his or her true heart to sin (see 2 Cor 5:17), whereas the lost person acts in accordance with what his or her heart desires.

Those who engage in affairs experience "warm fuzzy" pleasurable feelings and mistake them for love. Of course, there can never be love in an adulterous relationship, for how can agape (true love) and immorality coexist? The truth is, most people get married for the same reason they enter into an affair. They hope their future spouse will provide them with an ongoing supply of the "warm fuzzy" pleasure that they have felt while dating and have mistaken for love. This elation is stirred by the hope that the other person will fulfill some perceived need, take away some longing, resolve inner pain, complete that which is believed to be lacking, and so on.

Then they get married and fall "out of" love in a few years (or days) when their partner fails to come through with what they expected and believed they should have delivered. As a result, they may be tempted to turn to someone else outside the marriage and repeat the process.

Each partner will trigger the lie-based pain in the other person's mind. When this happens, the partner may look (feel) like someone from the past who has wounded him or her. This is when people start saying things like, "You are just like my mother," "You sound just like my father," and so on.

Just as sex is not the motivation for adultery, neither is it the motivation for sexual addictions. The sex addict is using sexual gratification as a means for covering a deeper painful emotion. Whenever the painful emotion is triggered, he or she looks to sexual gratification to cover the pain. After a time, this process becomes automatic and appears to be sexually focused addiction. Yet if you can uncover the lie-based emotion that drives the behavior and follow it back to its source, the person is in a good position to receive the truth, which can break the power of this so-called addiction.

Most addictive disorders have two primary roots. One is the physical addiction of the substance itself. Many people make abstinence the goal, but as I have already suggested, abstinence is not freedom. It is merely the cessation of an undesirable behavior by way of willpower, determination, and group support. People do accomplish abstinence through different programs, and I am in support of this effort, as abstinence is better than sinning, even though it is not freedom. Yet if the only thing a person does is abstain from his or her addiction, that person is a potential relapse waiting to happen. If a person's lie-based pain ever becomes greater than his or her resolve or if he or she loses his or her support system, that person will crumble, and there's a good chance that he or she will revert to the addiction or engage in another addiction.

The other primary root of addictive disorders is lie-based pain. Any time that a lie is triggered, it produces the same painful emotion the person felt the first time the event occurred. Somewhere along the way he or she discovered that drinking, smoking, overeating, drugging, or viewing pornography covered the pain.

We do what we do to avoid our deep-felt pain. We may have learned this means of coping from watching others in our family system, or we may have discovered it on our own. No matter how we discovered it, however, the addiction is not really our problem—in fact, it is our solution for pain.

Abstinence will resolve the physical cravings, for the most part, but it will not remove our emotional pain. If, however, we are willing to look at the source of our pain and discern its reason (the underlying lies), we can find truth. When we know the truth in our innermost parts, the pain will leave and the need to do the addictive behavior will no longer surface.

Paul came to us as a chronic alcoholic. He would stay intoxicated for weeks at a time. This behavior had cost him several jobs and was about to cost him his marriage. His wife had given up on him, was tired, and did not want to deal with him any longer. She had already moved out and refused to speak with him unless he got real help.

My schedule was full and I simply could not work him in, so my wife offered to minister with him. Sharon is not a trained counselor and does not profess to be. However, she has completed all the training that is offered through this ministry, and God is using her mightily as a lay minister. She began seeing Paul weekly for about two hours each session. It is important to note that she did not work on his drinking problem. She rarely mentioned it or asked how his "abstinence" was going. Sharon knew that his drinking was not the problem but rather his nonproductive solution for his emotional pain.

Each week she helped him find his way back to the deep wounds of his childhood. Paul discovered that as a teenager he had found "peace" for the first time by drinking. As Paul was willing to feel the pain and discern the lies he believed in these earlier memories, the Lord began to give him truth. As each truth entered into his mind experientially, he drank less. After a few months went by he reported that he was not drinking at all.

We saw Paul a couple of years ago. It had been over a year at that time since he had last seen us, and he had not had a drink. The exciting thing was that he said that he never thinks about it. When there is no pain, there is no need for a solution.

People remain addicted to alcohol or drugs, or maintain eating disorders, because lies remain embedded in their memories. Expel the lies and those suffering from these addictions will be emotionally free. With the passing of time in abstinence, these people will be physically free as well. I do not believe that "once an addict, always an addict." I do not remember the blind man Jesus healed saying, "Even though I can see now, I will always be a blind man." "Once a blind man, always a blind man" is a falsehood. The truth is that this man was once a blind man, but now he can see.

Finding Truth and Freedom

When we follow our present emotional pain back to its *source*, we will find a memory of something occurring that made us feel the same emotion that we are presently feeling. We can find truth and freedom in this place. Here the Spirit of Christ can reveal His truth to us. Christ removes the lie and replaces the painful emotion with peace. Theophostic Ministry is a process by which we can discern a person's experiential lie-based thinking and help him or her receive a freeing word directly from the Holy Spirit. When God replaces our lie-based thinking with truth, we can walk in effortless victory, which is maintenance-free. That's what Carla has discovered.

Carla's Story

Carla was an alcoholic attending four AA meetings a week. She was in abstinence but was daily battling the temptation to drink. Her marriage was on the brink and she was flirting with an extramarital relationship. She was on several medications for her mood swings and depression. She also suffered from an eating disorder, and had come to me for help with her present troubles. I asked her if she was willing to allow the Lord to take her to the memories where her present pain all began. She said yes. At first we had some difficulty getting to any memories, due to the dissociation in her mind.[4] However, as we processed through the dissociation, a painful reality began to emerge.

Her grandfather had molested Carla when she was between the ages of seven and nine. He would take her on special walks and trips. During the abuse, he would tell her that this was the way he expressed his love for her. He was very gentle as he performed oral sex on her. She was confused by this behavior and at the same time did feel a sense of being special. She also experienced feelings of sexual pleasure, causing even more confusion. After it was all over, she felt a deep sense of shame and guilt for what she had done with her grandfather.

As a young adult, she often felt deep self-loathing and shame, especially when she would try to be intimate with her husband. She had repressed the sexual abuse but could not suppress the emotional feeling coming from the repressed lies. Her eating disorder had brought her close to death due to malnutrition. She was physically worn out and an emotional wreck.

In our first session we discovered two basic lies in her thinking. One was that she was shameful and disgusting for "allowing" her grandfather to molest her, since she did not resist or try to stop him. A second was that she was a willing participant in the abuse because she felt pleasure during the ordeal.

This second lie was at the root of her eating disorder.[5] As a little girl, Carla discovered that if she focused on the pleasure she felt during the oral stimulation, she did not feel so overwhelmed by the shame and guilt of what her grandfather was doing. Yet afterward she felt shame because of the sexual pleasure she experienced.

During a Theophostic Ministry session, God gave her this freeing truth: He had created her body to experience pleasure, and her focusing on the physical pleasure was her way of getting through her grandfather's shameful act. God told her that she was not dirty or shameful for surviving. God's truth replaced her lie-based thinking and Carla's eating disorder ended, allowing her to progress on through her healing. Her lies had produced severe pain, which she had sought to manage through destructive behavior. As each lie was replaced with truth, Carla's present life calmed down, and she was able to walk in true peace.

We Can't "Put Our Past Behind Us"

Many people have tried to put their pasts behind them and not think about them any longer. This approach has never worked. However, this has not stopped the propagation of this false teaching, and as a result some Christians have been misled into believing that they should be able to leave their pasts behind them. Consequently, these Christians believe that something is wrong with them spiritually because they cannot lay their past wounds at the cross as they have their sins.

This teaching is based upon the statement of the apostle Paul in Philippians 3:13. This is probably one of the most misinterpreted Scripture passages, and is often used to defend the need to just "put our past behind us" (and, therefore, not do Theophostic Ministry). In it, Paul says, "I do not regard myself as having laid hold of it yet [the resurrection]; but one thing I do: forgetting what lies behind and reaching forward to what lies ahead...." To interpret this verse correctly, we must view it in context.

In this verse the apostle Paul is *not* referring to the wounding or negative experiences that have happened to him over the course of his life. As a matter of fact, he sees great value in the painful experiences of his life and alludes to them often in his writings. When he says he is putting the past behind him, he is not referring to his painful past, but rather the long list of great accomplishments of his life he has mentioned previously in this same passage. He provides a hefty list of his accomplishments and works in self-righteousness, and says he counts them as rubbish and is putting them all behind him. He says, concerning his life accomplishments,

> I myself might have confidence even in the flesh. If anyone else has a mind to put confidence in the flesh, I far more: circumcised the eighth day, of the nation of Israel, of the tribe of Benjamin, a Hebrew of Hebrews; as to the Law, a Pharisee; as to zeal, a persecutor of the church; as to the righteousness which is in the Law, found blameless. But whatever things were gain to me, those things I have counted as loss for the sake of Christ. More than that, I count all things [his accomplishments] to be loss in view of the surpassing value of knowing Christ Jesus my Lord, for whom I have suffered the loss of all things, and count them but rubbish in order that I may gain Christ.
>
> PHILIPPIANS 3:4-8

If we were to put this into contemporary language, it would read: "I am laying aside every degree, accomplishment, position, or status I have obtained in life that elevates myself or leads to self-righteousness and calling it all cattle poop compared to knowing Christ."

What is the substance of our thinking that needs to be renewed? Everything that is in our mind that is lie-based. What is the context in which this faulty, lie-based thinking resides? Our memories! If we put our past/memories behind us, then how are we ever to be renewed in our minds?

"Putting our past behind us" nullifies the command to be "transformed by the renewing of the mind" (Rom 12:2). Everything in my mind that is in need of being renewed consists of recorded memory. If I put my past (memory) behind me, then I cannot renew my mind.

"Putting our past behind us" fails to recognize that everything we do in the present is dependent on the past. Memory is the primary resource from which we live our present life. Everything we think, believe, and eventually choose to do is based upon the experiential knowledge in our memories. In order to be different ("transformed by the renewing of the mind") we must deal with our history. "Putting our past behind us" is nothing more than denial and fanciful thinking. It also reveals self-righteousness and works-salvation since "apart from Christ we can do nothing." It is no more possible for me to overcome my lie-based thinking apart from Christ than it is to overcome my sin. Salvation is a total work of Christ. It is not a "you and me, God," operation. "Putting my past behind me" is an attempt at healing myself of my historical pain through denial and repression.

"Putting our past behind us" is a noble gesture, but a neurological impossibility. When we do this we are simply suppressing our true pain. Suppression does not eliminate any aspect of the memory information in our minds. It simply buries it so that we cannot access it. Nevertheless, it is subconsciously accessed automatically when "triggered." Suppression allows emotional pain to be easily transferred into our present life while its true source (lie-based memory) goes undetected by our conscious awareness. Suppression results in our past not being acknowledged, while allowing the hidden lies to influence our present emotional state, resulting in wrong behavior.

"Putting our past behind us" fails to recognize that though we live in the present we are totally dependent on our past whether we want to admit it or not. Every present thought is connected or linked to our past at some level. This is simply the way that God designed our brains to work. To "put our past behind us" then, is to be in conflict with the way that God created our minds to work. Well-meaning pastors and teachers have taught us to deny our "old hurt and feelings" and put our memories behind us the same way we do our past life of sin. We are told to nail it to the cross and claim our victory. The sad truth about this admonition is that it does not work, never has, and never will. This teaching has simply left many wounded hurting people in bondage to their lie-based pain and in a perpetual cycle of defeat.

Because all of us are emotionally damaged at some level, putting our past behind us is not a good option. However, genuine healing is! Some of us deny and hide our lie-based thinking better than others, but we all need God's truth to find healing. It is not a question of whether we are wounded, but rather of how extensively we have been damaged.

The cross of Jesus was sufficient for all our sins and emotional wounds, but sins and wounds must be dealt with differently. The trouble is not in the effectiveness of the redemption, but rather in the application of the redemption. God has indeed redeemed us from our sin once and for all, but every day we are in the process of mind renewal as we are being exposed to the lies we believe and being given the opportunity to receive the truth that will release us of our emotional bondages. Until we find freedom from these lie-based wounds, we will struggle with the consequential sins these wounds manifest.

All of us are hurt by others and through life circumstances and at some point misinterpret things that happen. This misinterpretation is the lie-based thinking that cripples us in the years to follow. If my parents tell me that I am not "good enough," I will internalize this lie. Later, when anyone or anything triggers this thought, I will feel the same emotion as I did with the original wound. This emotional surge will be a primary motivation for the choices I make in each situation. Until the Spirit of Christ reinterprets this experiential lie, I will not be able to live out the reality that I am acceptable, righteous, made complete, since I am raised up with Him, and seated with Him in the heavenly places in Christ Jesus (see Eph 2:6).

Choose this day to find the freedom, peace, and joy that await you in Christ. "Stand fast therefore in the liberty by which Christ has made us free, and do not be entangled again with a yoke of bondage" (Gal 5:1, NKJV).

FOUR

Theophostic Ministry: The Renewing of the Mind

A Key Event in My Own Life

When I was in the fifth grade I used to ride home each night on the school bus. We lived about twelve miles out of town. A few days before Christmas break an unfortunate event occurred one evening while I was coming home on the bus. Our bus driver foolishly allowed some of us children to stand up near the door and in the stairwell as the bus was traveling down the highway. That evening as we were traveling down the highway, the door suddenly opened. Almost as quickly as it had opened, the driver shut it again and told us all to go to our seats. No one noticed that a little boy who had been standing on the bottom step had been swept out the door and was now lying near death in the ditch by the road. If a passing motorist hadn't discovered his broken body, the boy would have surely died.

The next day at school I was called down to the office, where a series of harsh and uncalled for interrogations took place. To this day I am not certain why I was questioned, but I was yelled at, accused of "attempted murder," and told that if the boy died (he was still in a coma) my parents would go to jail, along with other preposterous claims and accusations. The experience left me very wounded and filled with lies about my character and myself. I believed that I was guilty even though I wasn't. I believed that when bad things happened around me, people would blame me and think I caused them. I believed that I was somehow bad, though I was not really sure why. These lies impacted my childhood from that point forward. My grades went from As and Bs to all Ds and Fs. These lies followed me throughout my adult life, up until the last few years, when I personally received Theophostic Ministry concerning this memory.

For most of my adult life I did not know that my emotional reaction to certain situations was a triggered response of my mind going back to this particular memory. I did not know that the underlying illogical feelings of guilt I would often feel were coming from this event. I put as much effort as anyone else did into trying to find freedom through prayer, Bible study, and diligent determination. However, it has only been since I returned to that traumatic event in my childhood and found God's truth that I have been able to walk in freedom from the fears, anxieties, and emotional pain that these lies had created. As I have found genuine healing of my past in this area of my thinking, my present has been redeemed accordingly and I've found it possible to more fully appropriate the logical truths that I have cognitively accumulated.

Accumulation of Truth Is Not Enough

Our memories contain all the information that is stored in our minds. Everything we know, we learned in some life situation, and this presently makes up our reservoir of knowledge.

Our memories themselves do not need to be healed, since they are merely the containers of information. Rather, it is the false interpretations contained in our memories that need to be healed or corrected. The traditional approach to this has been through cognitive assimilation of new data. Many have believed that just receiving cognitive truth could release or change the lies a person believed. This approach has some merit, but for the most part it's simply inadequate.

As I have mentioned, I have worked with incest survivors for many years. In each counseling session, we would go to their memories, week by week, month by month, and often year by year, with few real results. I told these women the truth over and over, and yet they still carried some measure of residual pain from their abuse. The reason for this, which we will explore more fully later, is that people cannot change experience with data; we can change experience only with experience. Theophostic Ministry leads people to the place where they can experientially encounter the One who is truth: Jesus.

How the Mind Works

From infancy to adulthood our minds are gathering, assimilating, interpreting, and processing the information that they receive. We are either receiving information passively through gathering raw data such as "two plus two equals four," or receiving it experientially, through life experiences, such as being laughed at by our classmates because we wrote "two plus two equals five" on the blackboard by mistake. When information comes to us through experience, our minds couple it with some emotion. This emotionally charged information (whether positive or negative) becomes the primary source upon which we rely for future experiential decisions and responses. The nonexperiential logical data is passive and void of any real emotional quality, and is used in nonemotional situations, such as doing a mathematical calculation.

However, we draw upon the experiential information every time we encounter an experience that involves the same emotion. Once the original experience is recorded, with its emotional response and belief interpretation, it changes very little over time, even with the accumulation of additional data that is contrary. This original experience becomes the grid from which all similar additional life experiences are measured, interpreted, and emotionally experienced.

New experiences tend to confirm what was believed in the original event instead of reinterpreting or augmenting it. If my original experience was one of being abandoned, I might interpret this experience with a belief that says, "I have been abandoned because there is something wrong with me." This thought will produce emotions such as insecurity, self-hate, fear of rejection, and abandonment. When a new experience arises where I find myself alone again, I will begin with this same thinking and emotional response. I might say, "See, there is something wrong with me." Even if I learn new truth cognitively, such as, "God loves me and would never abandon me," it has little or no impact on the original, experiential belief that "I am all alone." I may be able to quote the Scripture, "I am with you always" (Mt 28:20) and yet still feel alone.

Problems arise for us when our new experiences are interpreted through the lens of older painful ones, which have nothing to do with the current experiences. The mind places the old interpretation over the top of the new experience and falsely interprets it. When this happens, the new experience will feel like the old, and we will react in the same way that we did in the original situation. This is the source of most relational conflict.

I said earlier that our beliefs about an event are what cause us painful emotions in the present; it is not the event itself. The event is over and the trauma is no longer happening, but the beliefs remain. If the traumatic event was the reason we were still in pain, then theoretically we could never be free, since the memory of the event will always be present in the mind. The event, however, is merely the container, which holds the belief or interpretation that was given to the event. This is why each time anything occurs that is remotely similar to an earlier traumatic event, we feel the original pain. The present "trigger" simply activates the lie-based thinking in our memory, which produces emotion, which matches the belief, which usually results in behavior. If I believe that I am dirty and shameful in a sexual abuse memory, then I will probably feel dirty and shameful when having sex with my marriage partner. I can logically know that I am not "dirty" during marital sex, yet still experience bad feelings if the lie-based memory is triggered by the present situation.

I remember watching the incest survivors in my group tremble in fear and abreact in pain as they revisited their memories of abuse. Some would gag and choke as though they were being orally raped. Why could they just not tell themselves the truth and go on? Their minds were holding on to that which was no longer true. No amount of effort on their part or mine could free them from the power of the lies they believed. Only a word from the Spirit of Jesus Himself could free them.

Most Inappropriate Behavior Is
Motivated by Lie-Based Pain

We are able to walk in freedom as we come into experiential truth from the Holy Spirit. This process is an intricate part of the total process of having our minds renewed. Discipleship, teaching, and personal Bible study all play a part, but these things cannot accomplish this task on their own. The primary purpose of mind renewal is to remove the barriers of deception that hinder us from knowing and experiencing the truth of who and what we presently are, as a result of the total and complete work of Christ. Every lie we accept hinders our view of the truth of who we are in Christ. Every lie produces matching emotions, which cripple our life and walk with God. If we believe that we are worthless and no good, we will feel the same and in turn act out in a manner consistent with this belief.

When I was a child I received a lie that what I did was always less than what it should have been. As an adult, the emotions that this lie produced drove my behavior. Some people who have accepted a similar lie become underachievers, feel defeated, and give up on doing anything or are slow to attempt things. I went in the opposite direction. I decided to prove that this was not true (even though I believed it was). Some might say that I did the right thing by choosing to try harder, accomplish more, and prove the lie wrong. Yet all my diligent effort did not remove one sliver of the power of the lie. I just became driven and a workaholic, never accomplishing enough to alleviate the pain.

My educational pursuit was a vain attempt to remove the pain caused by my lie-based thinking. I completed over one hundred hours of master's-level work in counseling and education and finished my Doctor of Ministry and most of the coursework for my Doctor of Education in marriage and family counseling before I began to discover the lies that were driving me. Today I am no longer driven by these lies. Jesus has released me (for the most part) and my family and I are grateful. The diplomas and degrees that I used to hang proudly on my walls (evidence to all that I was capable) are now packed away somewhere in our basement, along with so many other lie-based accomplishments. I'm not saying that educational degrees are not of value or important, I am simply saying that not all "good things" are motivated by truth or peace. Much of what we do is driven by pain.

From my own personal experience and from watching those around me in ministry, I believe that much, if not most, of the ministry that is being performed in churches, pastors' offices, and Christian counseling centers is motivated by people's pain more than by spirituality. I realize that I have just made a very big assumption and accusation, but let me explain.

I served in local Southern Baptist churches for over seventeen years before opening a private practice in counseling in the early 1990s. I operated this practice up into 1995, when I "burned out" and then discovered and began using the

Theophostic principles. During the first twenty years of my ministry I saw many good things happen in the lives of people with whom I ministered. People came to Christ, marriages were saved, and people became more spiritually and mentally functional and grew in knowledge and understanding of God and His Word. Yet as I look back at the emotion that was driving my work and ministry, I see underlying stress and anxiety. Some might see this as just a symptom of an "A"-type personality. However the truth is that a fear of rejection, a need for acceptance, feelings of inadequacy, and a fear of people (to mention just a few of my lie-based emotions) were what drove my behavior. The lie-based pain contained in my childhood wounds was the primary motivation driving my ministry efforts. God used my efforts to help many people, but my motive was not one of peace.

Somewhere under all this pain I had a heartfelt desire for people and their healing and growth, but my predominant driving force was lie-based pain. Yet—and here is the difficult part of all of this—I did not know that this was so until I began to allow healing to come into my own life through the principles in this book. I honestly believed that I was in good shape. I had already "dealt with" most of my life history, I had already forgiven those who had hurt me, and I had a good grasp and understanding of what was going on inside of me. Those around me saw me as confident, in charge, determined, focused, spiritually mature, grounded in the Word, and for the most part very well-adjusted. I can now see that I presented most of these traits as a protection from further pain.

What Is True Mind Renewal?

Mind renewal goes beyond the gathering of biblical facts and knowledge to the place where the believer is able to walk in the present reality of righteousness that he or she has already laid hold of in Christ. Lie-based thinking robs us of knowing this reality. My own efforts at and determination in overcoming sin do not make me more righteous or holy, but rather I am presently standing "holy and blameless before Him" in Christ (Eph 1:4). "If any man is in Christ, he is a new creature" (2 Cor 5:17). The reason that I do not always emotionally and experientially know this reality is due to the lies I believe. Yet as each lie is replaced with truth, I come to know who and what I am in Christ, and this reality becomes an effortless outflow of the truth I experientially possess.

I used to teach that we were in the process of becoming more and more like Jesus. I now realize that we are not becoming like Him—we are already like Him and can know this reality as we come to know truth. Some might suggest that this is simply semantics and actually saying the same thing. Yet theologically and practically these things are very different. If I am becoming something, then I am not yet fully that which I am becoming. This would imply that I have much work to do to achieve what is lacking. However, if I am a complete new man in Christ, then my new self does not fluctuate or vacillate, even though my emotional state may run contrary. I am not becoming something new, since I am already complete. As a new man, I am maturing and growing in knowledge of this reality, but my righteous state of being remains consistent. When I feel condemned, shamed, unloved, not good enough, and so on, my trying harder, being more determined, or performing better will not make me more of what I am in Christ, which is "holy and blameless before Him" (Eph 1:4). These contrary emotions are either the consequence of wrong choices I have been deceived into making (sin) or else they are symptoms of my false self-belief and therefore not my true spiritual condition.

We are often commanded in Scripture to "lay aside" sinful behavior (Rom 13:12, Eph 4:22, Heb 12:1). However, my motivation for laying aside my sinful behavior should not be that I might become more holy, righteous, or have a better standing with God, but rather because I *am* all of the above. My laying aside is not in order to become something but rather because I am something (Eph 1:4, Col 3:12, 2 Cor 5:21).

This is a major paradigm shift for the contrary thinking that has permeated the church. Whether we will admit it or not, much of what we call spirituality is nothing more than works salvation and a vain attempt to arrive at some perceived holy state. Anything that I believe will increase, sustain, or maintain any level of my righteous and holy place with God, is works and not grace. We have been deceived into believing that performance equals spirituality. This is just not so. Performance or effort do have a place in the Christian growth and maturity process, but have nothing to do with my spiritual condition.

Christian growth and maturity is growing in the knowledge of who we are presently in Christ through rebirth and grace. The reason we do not know or live this out is not because it is not a reality, but because the lies in our minds have blinded our eyes to this truth. Christian growth and maturity is a "revealing" of what we possess in Christ Jesus. I am in Christ and what I was before (lost, depraved, separated from God) has all passed away (in my spirit), where "all things have become new" (2 Cor 5:17, NKJV), whether or not I believe it, feel it, or experientially know it. My lies tell me I am shameful, guilty, imperfect, less than others, or unacceptable. God's Word says I am redeemed, righteous, and holy. Who am I going to believe?

I am in the process of coming to the place where what I experientially believe matches what I am in Christ. Wherever there are deception and lies, I will have difficulty appropriating my present righteous place in Him.

Suffering Exposes Lie-Based Thinking

Some people have suggested that I am advocating a life free of all pain. This is not true. What I am saying is that any emotional pain that is rooted in faulty, lie-based thinking is not God's will for anyone at any time. However, it is God's will that Christians suffer as a result of life situations or as an overt act of persecution. Peter affirmed suffering as God's will when he said, "let those who suffer *according to the will of God* commit their souls to Him in doing good, as to a faithful Creator" (1 Pt 4:19, NKJV, italics mine). The apostle Paul said that he was destined to suffer for Christ (see 1 Thes 3:3).

I am very aware and see the necessity of suffering in the life of the believer. As a matter of fact, suffering is God's primary tool for exposing my lie-based thinking. When the fire comes, I am exposed. If I know truth in my innermost part (not just logically and cognitively), I will remain in peace during the fire. If I believe lies, I will respond to the suffering through my lie-based thinking, and the painful emotions that match my belief will surface automatically. Paul's mind had been greatly renewed when he said, "I have learned to be content [at peace] in whatever circumstances I am" (Phil 4:11). James said that the proper response to suffering was joy: "Consider it all joy, my brethren, when you encounter various trials, knowing that the testing of your faith produces endurance" (Jas 1:2-3).

The Way to Perfect Peace

When what we believe at the experiential level matches the biblical truth we know at the logical level, we will walk in perfect peace. As long as we hold on to the lies of our experience, we will remain in a continual struggle between the lies we believe experientially and what we hold logically to be true. Paul said in Romans 12:2 that we need to be transformed in our minds. The next part of this verse tells us why: "that you may prove [manifest/live out] what the will of God is, that which is good and acceptable and perfect." God's perfect will is realized as we experientially stand "holy and blameless before Him" (Eph 1:4).

Ephesians 1:3-14 is a lengthy passage, but I want to encourage you to slowly read through what the apostle Paul is saying about our present condition and the relationship we possess in Christ. I have underlined some of the spiritual realities we presently possess and the tenses of the English verbs used in describing them. God wants us to experientially live in this reality, but our experiential lie-based thinking blinds the eyes of our heart from knowing these realities. My comments appear within the brackets.

Blessed be the God and Father of our Lord Jesus Christ, who <u>has</u> [accomplished task] blessed us with <u>every</u> [nothing more to give] spiritual blessing in the heavenly places in Christ, just as He chose us in Him <u>before the foundation of the world</u>, [this was long before we had any say in the matter] that we should <u>be holy and blameless</u> before Him [God's plan from the beginning was that we have a holy relationship with Him]. In love He predestined us to <u>adoption as sons</u> through Jesus Christ to Himself, according to the kind intention of His will, to the praise of the glory of His grace, which He freely bestowed on us in the Beloved. In Him <u>we have</u> [present tense] <u>redemption through His blood</u>, the <u>forgiveness of our trespasses</u>, according to the riches of His grace, which He lavished upon us. In all wisdom and insight He made known to us the mystery of His will, according to His kind intention which He purposed in Him with a view to an administration suitable to the fulness of the times, that is, the summing up of all things in Christ, things in the heavens and things upon the earth. In Him also <u>we have obtained</u> [present reality] an inheritance, <u>having been</u> [past tense] predestined according to His purpose who works all things after the counsel of His will, to the end that we who were the first to hope in Christ should be to the praise of His glory. In Him, you also, after listening to the message of truth, the gospel of your salvation—having also believed, <u>you were sealed</u> [a done deal] in Him with the Holy Spirit of promise, who <u>is given</u> as a pledge of our inheritance, with a view to the redemption of God's own possession, to the praise of His glory.

EPHESIANS 1:3-14, underlining mine

Then in verse 18 Paul goes on to declare the importance of having our minds renewed so that we might come to know these realities: "I pray that the eyes of your heart may be enlightened, so that you may know <u>what is</u> [present tense] the hope of His calling, <u>what are</u> [present tense] the riches of the glory of His inheritance in the saints" (underlining mine). As we find freedom from the lies stored in our memories, these truths can become an experiential reality.

This is why Paul declares in Romans 12:2: "be transformed [completely changed in behavior] by the renewing of your mind." Otherwise, we will have little choice but to be "conformed to the world." Until we are renewed in mind, we will never be able to know fully who we are in Christ. Every lie that God replaces with divine truth allows us to live more freely through our true present hearts of righteousness. As we come into the knowledge of who we are in Christ, we can appropriate the deeper things that result in the ongoing maturing of our inner person.

Experiential Knowledge and Logical Truth

Again, our memory contains two levels or types of information: logical memory and experiential memory. The logical data or truth is an accumulation of the data that we have gathered through nonexperiential or nonemotional means and is emotionally passive. For example, we may gather biblical information sitting in a class lecture or from our personal Bible study. We might learn about the faithfulness of God and how He is our protector and the source of all things that we need in life.

This information is true and has the potential to change our lives if we can experientially grasp it. We may even set out to apply this truth and discipline ourselves to do so. Never-the-less, this information is passively stored in our logical databases, apart from emotional experience. (Though the class setting is technically an experience, it does not usually require an emotional response.)

On the other hand, if later that night a mugger accosts us and robs us of all our money in a parking lot, we are gathering information that is experiential by nature. We might gather from this experience that God does not protect us, that this world is not a safe place, and that we walk in constant danger of being hurt. The mugger incident gives us experiential knowledge that we may interpret in a fashion contrary to what we learned logically in Bible class. In the days ahead, as we walk across campus, we will likely feel fear, cautiousness, and feelings of vulnerability, which come from our experiential knowledge. We might try to draw from our logical truth by quoting the passages of Scripture about God's protection, but we may still feel fear. Because we have learned this informa-tion experientially, our minds will rely more heavily on it than on the logical truth we learned in the classroom setting.

In like manner, when emotionally charged events occurred in our childhood, we interpreted them from the emotions we felt. These interpretations became our basic and guiding source of information for any future situation that was even remotely similar.

I'll say it again: in life situations experiential knowledge tends to override logical truth. We can choose to embrace log-ical truth in times of crisis, but generally we will submit to that which we "feel" is true rather than that we "know" to be true. This is why people who administer Theophostic Ministry ask the person undergoing ministry what "feels" true, as opposed to what is true. What we feel is an indication of what we truly believe. If we are in a nonthreatening environment like a Sunday school class, we will spout off the logical truth we have memorized. This "truth" is not necessarily what we operate from, however, when we are in a real-life situation.

As I mentioned earlier as a way of example, if we lose our jobs next week our feelings will expose our true beliefs. If we are overcome with panic, fear, and uncertainty, then we do not believe that "God shall supply all your needs" (Phil 4:19), even though we have the verse memorized. What we feel shows what we experientially believe. Our experiences dictate, for the most part, how we will act in the present. If we have lies embedded in our life memory experiences, we will be crippled in our perception and life choices.

Those who have suffered childhood trauma clearly show how one's experiential knowledge dictates one's present reality. If you have worked with survivors of sexual abuse, then the following scenario will be very familiar to you.

Mary was washing dishes when her husband came up behind her and gave her a gentle hug. Immediately she recoiled and reacted negatively to his embrace. In anger she scolded him not to do that. He was confused by her reaction, since all he had done was hug her. She could not explain why she reacted this way, but nevertheless she did not like what he had done. What happened? Mary's mind supplied her with experiential knowledge of past abuse. She felt the emotion and sensation of being held against her will, which she had learned in the childhood abuse. Logical truth could tell her she was presently safe and that her husband's hug was good, yet her experiential knowledge hindered her receiving and embracing the reality of this truth.

As Christians, we need logical truth in order to grow and mature in the Christian life, but this truth is difficult to appropriate if our experiential knowledge is contrary. If we believe the lie that says, "I am stupid and cannot do anything right," we will have great difficulty receiving and living out the truth that we are loved and acceptable to God. Our emotional responses to life situations will match our experiential belief system, not our logical database. It does not matter what we say or think we believe, because our emotions will expose our true belief systems when we are faced with real-life situations. What we believe to be true in a given situation will be evident by what we feel in that moment. If we say that we believe God supplies all our needs and is our Protector, yet we experience fear or anxiety in a given situation, then we really believe something different from this. Due to this conflict between logical beliefs and experiential knowledge, many of us struggle to live out our logical truth. Our logical data tells us that we are forgiven and that God accepts and loves us, but our experiential knowledge often condemns us.

Joan came to me depressed and with much body pain, which her medical doctor had diagnosed as fibromyalgia. I asked her if there were times when she felt more pain and depression than others, and she reported that she felt more pain at work than anywhere else. She said that she loved her work but that at the same time it depressed her. I asked her about her job and discovered that she was part of a ministry for unwed mothers. I asked her to feel the emotional pain she felt at her ministry, and then asked the Lord to take her to the source of the pain in her memory. Almost immediately she said, "But I have already dealt with that. I know that God forgave me for that!" Joan had had an abortion as a teenager, and had asked the Lord for His forgiveness while seeking counseling from a pastor many years before. So I asked her what she felt as she looked at the abortion memory. She began to sob, and said, "I feel so ashamed. But I know God has forgiven me. I just cannot understand why I still feel so bad. I guess I just cannot forgive myself."[1] Joan's logical truths about God's forgiveness and grace were right on target, but this had had little effect on her emotional state.

This scenario is common with people who have sinned in dramatic ways. They have sought genuine forgiveness and yet cannot find release from the pain. What was happening here was a conflict between what Joan's logical truth was saying and what her experiential knowledge was telling her. I asked Joan to embrace the pain she was feeling and to discern why she was feeling what she was feeling. She said, "I feel like a murderer. I killed my baby. How can God ever forgive me? But I know I am forgiven. I have confessed this terrible sin a hundred times and have asked Him to forgive me. Why can't I go on? Why do I still feel such shame?"

Years ago I would have pulled out my "Claim it by faith," "Reckon it to be so," and "Trust God, not your feelings" lectures. Today I said, "Let yourself feel the shame and embrace the thought that you are a murderer." I then continued with the Theophostic process and watched as the Spirit of Jesus began to experientially minister to Joan with truth. In just a few short minutes she looked up at me with a changed countenance, beaming with joy and release. She said through her tears, "He just said it was really OK. I am forgiven." Now Joan's experience matched her logical truth, and from here she was able to walk in effortless victory. In the past she had had to battle the shameful feelings and claim the truth even though it did not feel true. Now she could claim the truth and experience the peace and joy this truth afforded. By the way, Joan's body pain never returned after this session, and her doctor found no further signs of the fibromyalgia.

The body often expresses the conflict in one's thinking through physical pains and ailments. When our minds are at peace, our bodies frequently will heal themselves. When there is lie-based pain in our minds, our bodies often act out accordingly. I believe this is why we don't see more healing in the church today—the physical illnesses are lie-based and will not go away until the lies are removed. If my headaches are rooted in my lie-based thinking, God will not heal my headache. Yet He can give me experiential truth, and as a natural result my headache will go away on its own.

Change Experience With Experience

We can change data with data, but it requires experience to change experience.

People come to counselors and ministers for help for many reasons, but mostly it's for help with emotional pain. They may say they've come because of what is happening in their lives, but almost always the real reason is the historical lie-based pain they are feeling. Remember, we are not miserable or in pain because of what has happened to us, but rather because of how what has happened feels. When true healing occurs in a person's mind, the memories of traumatic events will still be intact, but the lies will no longer be attached to the memories, and consequently the pain associated with those memories will also be gone. Lies such as, "I am bad, no good, not lovable, rejected, abandoned, shameful, evil, and so on" cause us to feel bad, not what has happened to us. What we believe about what happened is what causes the pain.

Many counselors seek to change wrong beliefs by providing those they counsel with Scriptures or truth statements. They expect the wounded person to hear and receive the truth and then quit thinking the false thoughts and thereby feel better. Yet if we are honest, we know that this does not work. What happens is usually just the opposite. Now that the problem is exposed, many people feel even more defeated because they still cannot make themselves feel better even though they have been given the truth. This happens because we cannot change experience with new data. We can change data with data, but experience requires new experience to effect any real change.

For example, Sharon and I were on a trip to the Chicago area one day. We left our home in central Kentucky, taking Interstate I-65, which runs north and south. For those of you who may not know, Chicago, Illinois, is north of Kentucky, while Tennessee is the state that lies due south. Once we got on I-65, I set the cruise control, relaxed, and enjoyed conversing with my wife as we headed for Chicago. After a couple of hours, Sharon asked me, "Are you sure we are going the right direction?"

I responded as any red-blooded male would answer: "Say what? Of course, I know where we are."

A few more miles down the road, an extremely large and boisterous sign proclaimed the words, WELCOME TO TENNESSEE.

A person can be fully convinced that he or she is going the right direction and in reality be going completely the wrong way. However, this type of misinformation is based on logical truth and can be easily corrected. If I pull out my map and see the (logical) truth of how to get to my destination, I will immediately assume that the former directions were false and make the necessary corrections. This correction is immediately stored in my logical database, where I can avoid the same mistake, should I ever pass that way again. This logical adjustment is easy to make in this area of the mind (except for having to face my wife with my mistake), since this simply requires me to change data with data.

In contrast, however, it's not so easy to change what we believe experientially. More often than not, if you give a person new information that conflicts with what is stored in his or her experiential knowledge, that person will not even acknowledge the new information. He or she will subconsciously filter out the new information, since it does not match what is experientially believed.

Janice was a member of an incest survivors group I used to run. Before I began doing Theophostic Ministry, I used support groups to allow people with like problems to struggle together. This at least gave them a sense of not being alone. However, since using Theophostic Ministry, I have not had or needed such groups. People are finding release quickly, and groups are a thing of the past.

Anyway, Janice came each week to the group very depressed. She rarely fixed herself up before coming. Her hair was usually pulled back and her clothes seldom matched. Yet one night she came to group with her hair fixed up and a new outfit on. I immediately noticed and made a complimentary remark. Janice did not even look in my direction. I repeated myself, and she looked at me and gave me a very weak and cynical "thank you." I reassured her that I had meant what I had said, but I could see that she did not receive my words, so I asked her why she could not accept my compliment. She said, "I know that you really don't mean it." Yet, I did mean it, so I asked her how she had felt when I said the nice words to her. She gave me a strange look and said, "I know that what I am thinking is not true, but what I think is that you want sex. Men talk nice to me only when they want something."

Here is a good example of how one's experiential knowledge overrides incoming logical truth. This is why a preacher can deliver a powerful, truth-filled sermon that leaves his congregation neither touched nor changed. I have noticed in my own church that those who have found experiential freedom are more receptive to teaching, preaching, and discipleship. Perhaps we put the proverbial cart before the horse when we try to help people grow spiritually by filling their "cart" with more logical truth than their experiential "horse" can pull.

Go to the Gospels and read the stories of Jesus healing people. See how often He gave them an experience before He gave them the truth. Jesus healed the blind man without even talking to him first. Later, after the religious leaders in the temple had rejected the former blind man, he was given logical data about the identity of his Healer. Here the man with restored sight heard the truth from Jesus and believed Him to be the Messiah who had come (see Jn 9:32-33). I am not sure which must come first, the "chicken or the egg," but I do know that data and experience must both be present in a person's life in order for genuine change to occur. Biblical data without a genuine experience of God is powerless in bringing about genuine change.

Information that is emotionally stored in my experience will require a new experience to change it. This can happen only when the lie-based memory is replaced with experiential truth. Only the Holy Spirit can provide experiential truth to my historical experience. When the Holy Spirit reveals to the wounded person, "You are not alone," that person's experience changes. Yet if I had told that person, "You are not alone; God is with you," he or she would have agreed logically but still probably felt rejected. If we believe we are stupid and incompetent in our experience, very little new information will have an impact on what we have embraced as true. We can take a difficult test, score 100 percent on it, and we'll assume the test was flawed. If our friends and associates tell us over and over how competent we are, we will still feel just the opposite. Logical data has little power over what our experiences have taught us, yet many counseling offices, as well as the local church ministry, still often try to change our experiential lie-based thinking with such data.

The Problem With the 4-P Approach to Ministry

Most churches pray for people who come for prayer during an altar call, and often the one praying speaks words of encouragement and truths from the Bible. This, in and of itself, is a fine thing to do. Sadly, though, these prayers rarely result in a changed life. For the most part people return to their seats with the same emotional pain that they had when they came forward. Does this mean that prayer is ineffective in this context? Absolutely not! We must pray. However, I believe that if we do not address the core issues of a person's life, true freedom often eludes us. In this context we often make the mistake of trying to change experience with logical data.

As an example, I offer the following. It was a typical Sunday morning service at our church. We had experienced a good time of praise and worship and heard an insightful message, and the minister had asked people to come forward if they desired personal ministry. Several came forward and shared their needs with the pastor. Each one shared similar concerns, which pertained to some difficulty in their present life, accompanied by a measure of obvious emotional pain. The pastor, in turn, asked for people from the congregation to come forward to pray with those who had asked for ministry. A good number of people answered the call of the pastor, and soon prayers began to flow for those who had confessed their need. After a season of prayer the people all returned to their seats and the service drew to a close. I believe it was assumed by most people present that those who came for prayer were now in a better place spiritually and emotionally as a result of the prayers prayed by their fellow members. After the prayer time, they appeared to be less troubled and showed signs of being comforted and grateful for the expressions of concern that were offered.

As I watched the scene play out, I wondered what had really occurred in this common scenario. Did the emotional pain these people were feeling go away as a result of the prayer time? Did they go back to their seats renewed and in a different place than before the prayers were offered? What would they say to me if I asked them if the prayers had actually resulted in genuine release of their pain and the presence of perfect peace?

I've received answers to these very questions from people who have received prayers for their emotional pains. Based on these and my own experience of being prayed for, I have found that often not much change usually occurs. Sometimes we may feel better initially because of the affirmation and comfort we receive from others, but by the time we get to the parking lot, we are in the same place of pain we were before we went forward for prayer.

Does this mean that prayer does not work, is unnecessary, or is impotent? No, prayer does work—when it is applied within the proper context and in biblically supportive applications. Nevertheless, if these people are not truly helped through the prayers we pray, then why do we pray for them? It could be because we do not know what else to do. In any other area of life, work, or business, when what we are doing doesn't produce a desirable outcome, we reevaluate the practice, seek alternative approaches, and continue to try new things until we achieve the results we desire. Yet, people in the church often do the same things over and over, with little or no result, and make changes only as a last resort, and then rarely without the shedding of much blood.

Over the last twenty years there has been a new effort by many pastors and ministers to go beyond praying and become trained in counseling. Most seminaries now offer degrees in counseling. However, many ministers who have tried their hand at counseling find the trade-off costly, due to the enor-mous amount of time invested for often feeble results. Others have come to the conclusion (after many hours of working with the same people on the same issues, with little to show for their efforts) that counseling produces about as much fruit as trying to pray people's pain away. Most churches default to what I call the 4-P approach to ministry, which is "problem-pray-pretend-perform." It works like this: The person comes to the church with a *problem* or an emotional pain, which the church attempts to resolve through *prayer*. Once the prayers are offered up, the recipient is expected to *pretend* to be better by smiling, being grateful, and saying that he or she is better (when he or she usually is not). Then the person melds back into the congregational mold of *performance*-based spirituality.[2] If the person cannot pretend and perform, he or she is then recategorized by the church as unwilling to be healed, a carrier of some hidden sin he or she is unwilling to confess, not really saved, or maybe demonized.

If a person is considered demonized (the commonly assumed reason that the prayer was ineffective), some ministers apply the "4-P+D" approach, which adds *deliverance* of the demonic to the mix. Those who do deliverance ministry assume that the demons must be battled and cast out before the person can be free. Yet, casting out a demon does not make a person any freer of lie-based thinking than he or she was before, just demon-less. In most cases when a person comes for prayer for his or her pain and struggles, that person will simply default to suppression of the pain, pretending relief and performance for at least the amount of time it takes to get to his or her car in the parking lot.

I would like to suggest that we are taking the wrong

approach, at least in part. I am not saying that we should not pray for each other, for we must. However, we should look to the Scriptures and see how we are to pray, under what circumstances, and for what purposes, rather than using prayer as a "fix-all" approach to ministry. Maybe God doesn't intend for us to pray our pain and difficulties away. Maybe He wants us to find the true source of our emotional pain, face it, and embrace it, and in this context discover His truth and lasting freedom. Theophostic Ministry is a specific and focused prayer approach that moves people to the true sources of their pain and allows them to encounter Jesus.

As I sat in church that morning, watching those that had come forward for prayer, I was reminded of a poor fellow who was rushed to the hospital with acute appendicitis. He was in really bad shape. The church was alerted and the prayer team was sent in. They prayed for several hours over the man but his condition worsened. After a few more hours his appendix ruptured and his prognosis became grim. A second prayer team was called in, and they prayed fervently all the way up to the moment of the man's death. Since he was now in a better place (heaven), those praying assumed it must not have been God's will for this man to be healed. After all, they had done all they could do (pray). Can you see the problem in this story? The man had appendicitis! There is a common cure for the condition; it's called surgery. He did not have to die, since an appendectomy is a simple procedure (at least this is what I am told). A surgeon could have been called in, made an incision, cut out the infected part, and thereby removed the source of the illness. I am afraid that the church spends many hours praying for the healing of "appendicitis" when what we need is God's scalpel.

Some of you may be offended by my suggestion that there are applications where prayer alone is inadequate and exorcism is incomplete. Please don't misunderstand me. I am not saying that prayer is ineffective. Prayer is a vitally important biblical directive that we must do in the overall scope of ministry. Furthermore, I am not saying that exorcism is not a necessary part of a person's total ministry need when indeed it is called for and when a person is truly demonized. I have on rare occasions watched people being prayed for come into complete peace as the Spirit of God moved in powerful ways, releasing them of the pain and struggles in their lives without anything other than prayer being applied.

However, often people who receive prayer for emotional healing and help may feel loved and encouraged, but they often remain in pain. I hope that the church will make an honest appraisal of the outcome of the ministry it offers wounded people. Are people permanently moving from pain to peace in the areas of their lives for which they come to the church for help? We, as a church, have misinformed the wounded when we have communicated that if they would come with their pain and allow us to pray, things would get better. We may not actually say these words, but if our response to others' troubles and pain is merely "praying them through to victory," we may be forcing them to apply the 4-P method of relief.

Who Needs Emotional Healing?

People often ask me how many people I think are in need of emotional healing. My answer is, "Everyone raise your right hand." All of us need emotional healing. Not one of us is exempt. We all have lies in our thinking and minds that need to be renewed. As I have already said, it really is not a question of who needs ministry and healing, but to what extent we need it and how extensive the damage is. We are all emotionally wounded, but in varying degrees. Every person sitting in every church everywhere (in the pews and especially behind the pulpit) carries emotional pain at some level. You might think that you are OK and that you do not have any lie-based thinking. You may not have been abused or hurt in any significant manner as a child, and may even have been raised in a warm, loving, and spiritual home. Nevertheless, you have not made it this far without picking up lies.

Think over the last few weeks. Were there any moments in which you were frustrated, stressed, angered, worried, anxious, taxed, upset, fearful, hateful, argumentive, defeated, or pressured? If so, there was probably a lie at the source of these emotions. You may argue that you had a right to feel this way, or that your feelings were normal reactions to the situation. Yet, the Bible is clear that we are to be ruled by the peace of Christ. If we feel an absence of His peace, we are not walking in truth. What if you could have faced those same life experiences and felt peaceful rather than stirred? You can—if you choose to look inward and allow the Spirit of Christ to reveal to you His truth.

The church has been led to believe that good behavior equals spiritual maturity and that keeping our pain hidden (even from ourselves) is a virtue. Everywhere I go, I find the church is basically the same: a building filled with deeply wounded people trying hard to pretend that everything is well. Many of us sing, "It is well with my soul" (and indeed it is in our new hearts), but our minds are in pain. We stand and proclaim "Victory in Jesus" and "Standing on the Promises," while we live in secret defeat and emotional bondage. We call abstinence from sinning victory, when it is not. At some level we all need release from the lies we believe.

Emotionally wounded people can be healed and can find peace and freedom—but not everyone who needs healing is lining up for his or her portion. I have worked with people who knew they were in pain and claimed they knew the reason for the pain yet never sought release. They chose to hold on to a lie that said the reason for their pain was due to outside sources (people, situations, etc.) and an unwillingness to look inward.

Ann came to me complaining of a troubled marriage. She said she had already filed for divorce and had no plans of stopping the process. The only reason she had come for ministry that day was out of respect for her husband's last request before she ended the marriage. She told him she would come one time, but did not plan on coming a second time. I asked her what she felt the trouble was in their relationship.

I was surprised by her response. She said she had a good husband. He was more than she could have ever wanted or asked for. He was attentive to her every need, he was romantic, he talked to her, and he paid careful attention to family matters. She had only one complaint. She said that every time he came near her sexually, it made her skin crawl. She felt overwhelmed and trapped. She did not feel it was fair to him for them to go on in this manner, and wanted a divorce.

I asked her to focus on the feeling she felt when her husband approached her sexually. Her face began to contort with disgust. I asked her to disconnect from the picture of her and her husband but to stay focused on the painful emotion that had surfaced. Then I asked the Lord to take her to the place where she had felt this same emotional pain for the first time. All of the sudden she opened her eyes with a startled look on her face.

I asked her what she was remembering. With some resistance she finally shared the painful story of her sexual abuse as a child. The problem was not her dislike of sex, or what her husband was doing with her sexually. Her unhappiness with sex came from lies, which had been planted during her sexual abuse years earlier. The lies from her history had infiltrated what could have been a very happy and healthy marriage. However, as is sometimes the case, this woman left the session unwilling to deal with her memory, face the lies, and chose not to believe that these feelings toward her husband could be from her past. She made the decision to leave the marriage. The last report I had from her was that the same issues had surfaced in her new relationship. The new man in her life triggered the same pain, because the pain was not in the relationship but in her lie-based memories.

Ann's story underlines the necessity of embracing the trauma of our lives. We can bury the memory, but its pain will eventually surface, causing more problems. I have no doubt that if this woman could have embraced the reality of the abuse in her life, felt its pain, and received truth from the Spirit of Christ, she would have experienced His perfect peace and saved her marriage.

If your marriage is in trouble, I have hope for you. However, it will require you to stop blaming your spouse and be willing to go to the original places of your pain. If you are willing to do this, Christ can meet you there and you can find His perfect peace and release.

For whatever reason, most people believe that counseling or ministry is only for those deeply troubled. If you are seeing a counselor or minister, you may be seen as one of those who just can not "get it together" on your own. I hope that what I am writing in this book helps to tear down this falsehood and opens the door for all people to begin a healing or mind-renewal journey. We are all lie-infested and in need of release.

I want to encourage you to slow down a bit and become emotionally aware throughout your day. Notice when and what stirs you up emotionally in negative ways. What is it your spouse says or does that gets to you? What is it about your work that causes you to feel bad? Too often we just respond from our pain, while we instantly justify our pain-driven behavior. We are called to walk in inner peace. Peace is a natural by-product of experientially knowing truth. You feel what you believe: when you know truth in your innermost parts, you will have the perfect peace of Christ.

FIVE

When God Heals ...

Are People Really Being Healed?

Perhaps you're wondering, *How can I know for sure that people are truly finding release and healing through this method? Can real recovery from traumatic memory be lifted in a single healing moment? How do I know it will last? How do I even know if the memories people are reporting are true? How can I be certain that what is happening through Theophostic Ministry is truly of God?* Before we explore these questions more fully, let's reflect on the reasons they are raised in the first place.

Early on, no one questioned the validity of this ministry more than I did. I was skeptical, even though I was standing in the middle of what I am now convinced was God doing the miraculous. Over and over I witnessed God help the emotionally "lame and blind" to "walk and to see." I saw people consistently come to a place of rest in the presence of Jesus as He revealed His truth into their pain-filled memories. My limited view and experience could not comprehend this. I wondered if the changes I witnessed would last, if this method could be transferred to other counselors and ministers, and if it could be applied outside the context of what I was doing in other fields of ministry. Could I be certain that God was the source of the messages the people were apparently receiving? I had always believed (logical data) that God could do miracles in the world today, yet I was having trouble with His doing them in my own life and ministry. Miracles were something God did on special occasions—not every day.

I was seeing people find genuine peace in their places of pain. People were finding true release, session by session, as they were receiving His truth. As I continued to witness what seemed to be instantaneous recovery from lies rooted in painful memories in a person's life, I slowly let go of my skepticism and began to embrace what has become for me a very reliable and effective ministry tool.

I was seeing people enter into perfect peace, draw closer to God, and experience Jesus in a real and meaningful way. How could this be deception?

Simon was sexually abused at the age of five by his father. The abuse occurred only once, yet it left deep wounds of shame and confusion in this young man's life. During his first session with me, we discovered two lies that had been implanted in his mind during the abuse: *I am dirty and shameful for allowing my dad to touch me,* and *I am bad because I waited so long after the fact to report it.* I led this young man through Theophostic Ministry, and he immediately reported complete peace as he received healing truth from God. All the shame and guilt were gone. The next week he returned for his second session. We began by looking again at the original memory of abuse. I asked Simon to look for anything that did not feel completely peaceful and calm. I watched as he searched through the memory, looking for pain. He found none. The pain, shame, and guilt were still gone. Halfway through the session, Simon asked if we could end the session early because he had other things he needed to do. Emotionally crippled the week before, Simon now claimed he was completely free of the pain with which he had come in.

If I had met Simon before I developed Theophostic Ministry, I likely would have worked with him for years as I tried to get him to restructure his thinking and habitual behaviors. No longer. When a person receives truth in his or her lie-based memories, that person's dysfunctions simply go away. This is really not all that difficult to understand, if indeed the dysfunctional patterns are the person's attempt to deal with his or her pain. Remember, sin patterns, compulsions, addictive behaviors, and other disorders are usually people's solutions for pain rather than their problems. For example, if you came to me for ministry as a person suffering from an eating disorder, such as anorexia, I would not try to get you to start eating. I could tell you that if you did not eat, you would die, but you would already know this. I could tell you that you were "skin and bones," but you would not believe me. If I tried to make you eat, you would resist me, since refraining from eating was your "solution" and not your perceived problem.[1]

I might ask how it made you feel to think about eating a meal, and then I might describe the potatoes, gravy, and roast beef and ask you how my description made you feel. This usually stirs up the very emotions that the anorexia is masking or seeking to resolve. You might tell me, "To eat makes me feel out of control," or, "I feel afraid, powerless, angry, and helpless." Yet, once the lies producing these emotions are removed, the need for the "solution" will go away. When you know the truth, experientially, you will no longer need your "solution" and will let go of the disorder. (I have had very good success in working with those with eating disorders, as have many others around the world doing Theophostic Ministry.)

When Archie came to see me, he had no apparent disorder. His parents hadn't abused him and he'd not experienced any serious trauma, yet he was still in emotional pain. He was suffering from daily anxiety over his finances. He had come to me the year before I began using Theophostic Ministry, and we had "logically" worked through his financial situation, showing him that he had no reason to fear, yet his fears remained. I had thought the information I had provided would calm the fear and enable him to move on with his life. It didn't. In fact, when he came to see me again, he said his anxiety was worse than it had been the year before.

Like all of us, he carried a variety of lie-based thoughts that he had picked up throughout childhood. Archie experienced an incredible amount of healing during his first Theophostic Ministry session with me, and came back for a follow-up session the following week. In this session he excitedly reported that he had experienced no anxiety over his finances all week. He could no longer access his fear over finances. No matter how hard he tried to surface the fear and anxiety, he could not.

As I mentioned earlier, in the beginning I was very skeptical of what was happening during these Theophostic Ministry sessions. I came up with three questions to help me discern whether God was doing a work of healing in a person who had received Theophostic Ministry.

- Is the message received from God during the session biblically consistent?
- Does the person demonstrate the presence of the perfect peace of Christ in the memory that has been renewed?

- Does the person have genuine compassion and forgiveness for those who have hurt him or her?

Is the Message Biblically Consistent?

The "truth" the person reports receiving must be tested and challenged for biblical consistency. The Spirit of Christ will not give a message that is contrary or additional to what has already been given in the Scriptures. This is not to say that the message will always be a direct quote from Scripture, but the message will not conflict with Scripture.

For example, a person might report hearing the Lord say, "You are not alone. I am here with you," in a memory of a time when he or she had been abandoned. These words are consistent with Jesus' words: "I am with you always, even to the end of the age" (Mt 28:20). If the message received is not consistent with Scripture, then it is not valid. This "truth" should be rejected because it is not from God.

One day I was working with a woman who was reporting a memory of her father beating her mother. She saw herself hiding behind a table, watching helplessly, in terror of what was happening. She was fearful that her mother was going to be killed and that she would be all alone, without protection from her dad. The mother did not die and the father never hurt this woman, yet she still felt this fear. I asked the Lord Jesus to reveal to her His truth, and she told me, "He said that it was OK for me to be afraid. He also said for me not to think about this anymore. He said I should think about the good things my father did and put this memory behind me." This message violates Scripture. God's Word says, "perfect love casts out fear" (1 Jn 4:18). Therefore, it is not "OK to be afraid." Furthermore, not thinking about such things is denial.

Messages that are contrary to biblical truth may come from the person's own thoughts and conclusions. Other times they may originate from deceiving spirits who are seeking to confuse or hinder the healing. A person administering Theophostic Ministry must discern the validity of the reported message. This is why the minister must "be diligent to present [himself] approved to God as a workman who does not need to be ashamed, handling accurately the word of truth" (2 Tm 2:15). To be effective, the minister must be biblically knowledgeable and growing daily in God's Word.

Andrew came to me defeated in his Christian life due to his addiction to pornography on the Internet. He had struggled for years with lust and with occasional impulses to buy pornographic magazines, but with free access to hundreds of thousands of hard-core pornographic web sites, most of the time he gave in to his impulse. Andrew was part of a support ministry that helped him abstain from his addiction, but he told me that his mind was tormented with flashes and images of what he had already experienced.

Theophostic Ministry addresses pornography addiction differently than do most other approaches, because it doesn't see addiction to pornography as the root problem, but as the person's "solution" for lie-based pain. Some ministries see pornography solely as a sin problem that needs to be confessed, repented of, and somehow overcome. The truth is that this latter approach has had little success, since it is based on self-effort and willpower.

Andrew was trying to solve his emotional pain by calming and distracting it with pornography. Genuine freedom would never be found in self-sustained abstinence. He was surprised when I told him this. I explained to him that in order to find genuine release he must first identify what was driving the behavior (emotional pain) and then follow this pain back to its true source. When the memory source was discovered, the next step would be to discern what was believed in the memory that was producing the pain, and to allow Jesus to reveal His truth to the Andrew in the memory.

I asked Andrew what he felt just prior to going to his computer to view the pornography. I was not surprised when he told me he felt sexually aroused, even though I knew that this was not the truth (though he thought it was). The sexual arousal he felt was his solution to his pain. So I asked Andrew to think about what he felt just prior to feeling sexual arousal. He thought for a moment, but eventually he began to tear up. With a trembling voice he began to speak of deep pain of abandonment and rejection he had felt since early childhood. We asked the Lord Jesus to take Andrew to the first time he had felt these same deep, painful feelings. We soon ended up in painful childhood experiences, and here we discerned the lies behind Andrew's pain and invited Jesus to release him of this bondage.

Andrew began to hear a deceptive message, which he assumed was from the Spirit of Christ: "You must battle this problem, but if you do not give up you will win." This may sound noble, but it isn't biblically consistent. We do not have to battle sin. Jesus took on our sins on our behalf so that we could become free from sin. This was actually a message from a demonic spirit trying to keep Andrew in the cycle of defeat (defeat-confess-repent-adjust-perform). This lie was exposed and rejected, the demons were silenced, and soon Andrew received biblically consistent truth from the Holy Spirit, which released him of his emotional pain and resulted in true peace. After a few more sessions and many painful memories, Andrew reported complete release from any desire to view pornography. Remember, true freedom and victory require no effort on our part to maintain.[2] Andrew said that he found it easy to abstain from pornography when the pain was removed, since he really did not want to do it anyway.

Another time, a person reported to me that God said that the reason she was feeling so badly was because she had been sexually abused. She received this message prior to having surfaced any memories that suggested such was the case. I suggested that what she had heard was not truth but a deception of some kind. I never accept this sort of message as being from God, because God does not tell us the content of our memories apart from our own self-discovery. Instead, He allows us to uncover them as we have the capacity and the willingness to embrace them. You see, the mind forgets nothing, but at times it chooses (subconsciously) to put things in places where we do not see them with our conscious minds. They are not lost, just filed away so that we do not have to reconnect to them consciously. When we are ready to know the truth of what has happened to us, we will remember.

Does the Person Demonstrate the
Perfect Peace of Christ?

If a person has received truth from Christ in his or her lie-based memory, God's perfect peace will always be present. The apostle Paul taught, "Let the peace of Christ rule in your hearts" (Col 3:15). Peace always follows the Holy Spirit's message of truth. Lies steal our peace, while truth is a basis for our peace.

A person who administers Theophostic Ministry seeks to move a person ever deeper into his or her sources of pain until Christ's truth replaces the lies, resulting in His perfect peace. Such peace rarely, if ever, comes simply because the minister gives the wounded person truth in a logical instructive context. If cognitive truth resulted in peace, our churches would be full of peace-filled people. Christians today have more truth than any generation in the history of the church, yet many do not walk in perfect peace. A lack of peace indicates that there is a lie held in experiential memory. The memory needs to be searched further until all pain producing lies are replaced with God's truth and the person has the perfect peace of Christ.

If a person reports what appears to be biblically consistent truth and yet the pain remains and peace continues to be elusive, I've found that this truth is probably coming from the person's logical database of truth. Again, the truth has to be experientially provided by the Holy Spirit to bring about genuine release of lie-based thinking. Freedom is a God-initiated and -accomplished task, "for it is God who is at work in you, both to will and to work for His good pleasure" (Phil 2:13).

Some may think I am minimizing preaching, biblical instruction, and personal study. This is not the case. All I am saying is that it is the Holy Spirit who "leads us into *all* truth." We may hear a spiritually rich sermon but unless the Holy Spirit implants this truth experientially into our heart and mind, it is only recorded as data and logical information.

Theophostic Ministry is a systematic means of helping people to position themselves at the feet of Jesus so He might do all He has promised. In a sense, it is helping people to listen. "Let him who has ears hear what the Spirit says" (often stated in the New Testament).

Does the Person Have Genuine Compassion and Forgiveness?

Before I started doing Theophostic Ministry, I would work people through their mental barriers, appeal to Scripture, have them push through their anger and other revengeful emotions, and lead them through my formula prayer of forgiveness. After the prayer I would have them claim "by faith" that they had forgiven their offender, even though they often did not feel different. Even those that did have an "experience" by praying the prayer with me usually had difficulty later.

For example, a fellow came to me who hated his father for the bad things done to him when he was a child. I showed him what the Bible said concerning forgiveness, and led him to confess his hate and to "choose" to forgive his father. He did, and was relieved until the family reunion a few months later, when he saw his father. As soon as his father walked into the room, this man felt a wave of resentment surface.

Did he really forgive his father? Or did he just need to claim forgiveness by faith, deny his feelings, and act out the truth? I believe that he did forgive his father, but the resentment surfaced because he had not dealt with the true source of his pain, which was lie-based thinking held in memory. He lacked peace not from being unwilling to forgive but because he hadn't identified the lies producing the pain and received Christ's freedom in truth. Forgiveness releases a debt, but does not always release us from our lie-based emotion.

Since I began using the Theophostic Ministry model, I have watched many people genuinely forgive those who have offended them. Forgiveness is a natural by-product of receiving personal release from lie-based pain. When people truly find release of their lie-based pain, forgiveness and compassion for their offenders are natural outcomes.

I remember a young woman in her midtwenties who was emotionally devastated from being raped a few years earlier. This event had taken her emotionally out of commission and was ruining her life. Apparently, she had been abducted from a parking lot at gunpoint and harshly raped. The man showed no regard for her life and repeatedly threatened to kill her if she ever told what had happened. She was filled with terror and with rage and bitterness toward the rapist.

During a session with me, she was willing to revisit the rape memory. Hate, anger, rage, fear, shame, and feelings of abandonment surfaced. We identified many different lies that she had attached to the memory, such as, "The rape was my fault," "I should have told someone," "He is going to hurt me again," and "I am dirty because of what he did to me." As she

embraced each of these lies, the Holy Spirit revealed the following truths: "You are innocent; it was not your fault. You are
safe now. You are not dirty because of what he did; rather, he
defiled himself." When she heard these words, the perfect
peace of Christ permeated her mind and heart. I asked her if
any negative emotions remained in the memory. She looked
inside for a moment and then reported, "All I feel is release
and peace, with a little sense of sadness."

I assumed that she was referring to the sorrow and grief she
felt for herself for having gone through such an atrocity, and
replied, "It is normal to feel this way about yourself for this loss
you experienced."

Surprised, she said, "Oh no, I do not feel this for myself. I
am OK. I feel fine. I can look at that memory and all I feel is
peace and release from all the bad feelings. I just really feel
sorry for that man. He must have been very lonely and hurting to have come to the place to do what he did to me."

This woman felt true compassion and forgiveness. I never led
her through any prayer of forgiveness. I did not have to point
her to my favorite Scripture passages on forgiveness. I did not
have her accept her bad feelings after the prayer "by faith," or
"reckon" anything to be so. She was free, just like the king who
"felt compassion and released him [the servant] and forgave
him the debt" (Mt 18:27). Forgiveness and compassion are natural by-products that result when lies are replaced with truth.

Sometimes a person finds complete peace in the memory,
receives biblically consistent truth, and yet cannot find the
compassion from which to forgive the person who has hurt
him or her. This doesn't necessarily indicate that healing has
not occurred in the memory. More likely, the person's inability

to find compassion is due to other lies still present in other memories. We must discover the specific reasons for our anger, rage, resentment, and lack of forgiveness.

Too often people are led or manipulated to pray blanket prayers for all of their anger or inability to forgive. Yet, how can we forgive if we do not know why we need to do so? In Matthew 18 it says the king "took an account" of what the servant owed him before he forgave him. We are specifically hurt, angry, and resentful, and it is in these specific places that we must find release. We are angry for specific reasons in specific places. If we are going to find true release, we must visit those specific places and receive truth from the Holy Spirit *in each one.* Once we receive His truth and find perfect peace, we will also experience genuine compassion for those who have hurt us—even our abusers.

Much of what we have been taught about forgiveness is really nothing more than suppression of our pain. It doesn't work to simply just choose to forgive and "let it go." This is suppression and denial of the pain within. Genuine forgiveness is possible only as we find release from the emotional pain held rooted in our lie-based thinking. When we find His peace we can then experience compassion and truly "let it go."

Additional Evidence of Genuine Healing

As I have watched hundreds of people find hope and release from their lifelong pain and struggle, I have observed the following:

True Healing Is Permanent

I used to fear whether this dynamic change in people's lives could really last. If so, how long would it last? Would it fade away with time, like a posthypnotic suggestion? Would they have a relapse? When I first began to use Theophostic Ministry I had a secret fear that everyone who had received healing would one day come back in worse shape than when they had first come for ministry. This fear has proved unfounded.

Sometimes people will come back a week after healing and report that they are having more bad feelings. They sometimes assume that they are regressing or that they didn't receive healing. Yet in every case thus far, the "return" of the old feelings has meant that the memory contained additional lies that were missed or had not yet surfaced.

True Healing Results in Lifestyle Change

I am sure it was incredible for the blind man to receive his sight the day Jesus touched his eyes, but even more remarkable was the way his life surely changed from that moment forward. After his healing he would not be found down by the city gates, begging; now he could go down to the local employment office and apply for a job. Those who receive healing from their emotional memories no longer have to live in their crippled state. When the blind man received his sight, he did not have to work at seeing. When the emotionally crippled receive their "legs" back, they do not have to practice feeling peaceful and calm in those areas of their thinking. They will "feel" what the truth says. We feel what we believe.

True recovery means that we are free from the old pain and

lies. True recovery is deep inner healing that transforms naturally, without effort, into our daily walks and behavior. Once the lies are removed from our experiential knowledge and we find perfect peace, we are in a place where we can appropriate the Word of God in our lives.

True Healing Impacts One's Present Relationships

People often come to counseling because of the problems they are having with other people. They think, *If I am upset then you must be my problem, since you are in the room when I feel badly.*

Remember, however, our present conflict is rarely the source of our emotional pain. If a person is willing to put the present situation "on hold" in order to receive healing for the historical wounds in his or her life, that person can find peace and release in the midst of the current problem. When this happens, that person's perspective of the present can change. What was troublesome before often becomes more manageable, and sometimes entirely free and clear. The issues that kept the person stirred up and dominated his or her current life vanish along with the historical lies.

You can be free and can walk in peace, whether people around you change or not. You may be surprised at how many people stop doing what they do when you are no longer stirred up by it.

Now and then one of my twin daughters comes to me upset because of what her older brother is doing to her. I sometimes say, "The only reason he does what he does is because he knows it gets a rise out of you." The same is true in our adult relationships. I do what I do because you respond the way you do, and then I respond to your response. I trigger your pain, and your painful response triggers my pain. Change in either one of us can stop the cycle.

I remember one night, before I had the opportunity to access some of my lies and gain the measure of freedom I now know, Sharon asked me a question about my work. I felt attacked by her question, though now I realize there was nothing malicious in her statement. Still, I responded from my pain and she responded from her wound. We cycled our individual woundedness back and forth until we both were thoroughly exasperated.

However, since Sharon and I have been freed in this area through Theophostic Ministry, this particular cycle no longer emerges. Where there is no trigger, there is no pain, and when there is no pain there is no conflict. If you have to "work at" having a happy marital relationship, your effort is a good indication that you have wounded memories containing lies that need to be expelled and replaced with truth. When we were dating, Sharon and I didn't trigger each other's lies, and our relationship was easy. Once the lies surfaced, we had to start working at loving each other. Now that the lies have been replaced with truth, we can share genuine love for each other. We both are choosing to go to our places of pain and to find truth. Every place we find truth and experience God's peace, we no longer have any conflict with each other. If we cannot trigger each other, we do not have conflict. We do have differences of opinion, but these situations can be approached without the pain of the past.

True Healing Is Maintenance-Free

As we have already discussed, tolerable recovery usually requires an ongoing effort to maintain, and relapse threatens constantly. Yet true healing is accomplished through what God does, not through our own efforts. If we do not do anything to affect a change, we cannot do anything to maintain it, either. Healing is much like salvation of our spirit. It is "by grace are ye saved through faith;... not of works [self-effort], lest any man should boast" (Eph 2:8-9, KJV).

I used to ignorantly misinform survivors of sexual abuse and other traumas that they would have to learn to compensate for the emotional damage they had received from their abuse, since they could never know complete healing. I tried to instill a sense of hope by telling them a story of a man who had lost his legs in an auto accident, who, while he would never walk again, could live a productive life as he learned to compensate in other ways for his losses. I led them to believe they would get better, but that they would have to learn to live with the permanent damage done by the abuse. I no longer believe this.

Real healing does not require compensation. If I am recovered, then I am recovered. If I am healed, I can take up my bed and walk, not crawl or limp around in compensation. I now often see people who were emotionally lame take up their beds and walk when God reveals His truth in their lie-filled memories.

Remember that abstinence is rooted in self-control and self-effort, but healing and renewal are acts of God. Abstinence is a constant battle maintained by self-control. If I am struggling not to do something, then I am not experiencing victory.

God didn't ever expect us to keep the law. The law exposed and condemned each of us because by it no one could ever be justified.

For as many as are of the works of the Law are under a curse; for it is written, "Cursed is everyone who does not abide by all things written in the book of the Law, to perform them." Now that no one is justified by the Law before God is evident.... Christ redeemed us from the curse of the Law, having become a curse for us—for it is written, "Cursed is everyone who hangs on a tree"—in order that in Christ Jesus the blessing of Abraham might come to the Gentiles, so that we might receive the promise of the Spirit through faith.[3]

GALATIANS 3:10-11, 13-14

Since we are no longer under the Law, sin has no power over us. However, when our pain is stirred, we will look for a means of dealing with what is stirred up which often means sinful choices and behavior. Even though experiential truth from God is our only way of escape, most people look in other places to resolve it. Some look to pleasure, addictions, work, and relationships, while others seek to deflect it through blaming others, life situations, and even God.

We need to renew our minds so that we are not drawn aside by the lust of the flesh, which wages war with our minds (see Rom 7:23).

As we are renewed in our minds we will be filled with the knowledge of His will in all spiritual wisdom and understanding, freeing us to walk in a manner worthy of the Lord, to please Him in all respects, resulting in the bearing fruit in every good work and increasing in the knowledge of God; strengthened with all power, according to

His glorious might, for the attaining of all steadfastness and patience; joyously giving thanks to the Father, who has qualified us to share in the inheritance of the saints in Light.

COLOSSIANS 1:9-13, author's paraphrase

You really can know the "peace of God, which passes all comprehension" (Phil 4:7) and walk in genuine victory, and you can release those who have hurt you. I say this because I have found peace in places that I had never known peace before as I have allowed the Spirit of Christ to lead me into places that I did not want to go in my memories and have felt the pain those memories contained. I have found peace in every memory that I have visited, and look forward to the freedom that is still yet to come.

In summary, genuine healing will exhibit characteristics that demonstrate its validity. The healing will be permanent and will require no maintenance to sustain it. It will result in lifestyle changes and enhanced personal relationships. The final outcome will be the presence of true companion and forgiveness of those who have hurt us. Forgiveness is not something we have to work at, but rather is a natural by-product of genuine healing and resultant compassion. If we can't forgive, it's merely evidence that there are still areas of lie-based thinking from which we need to find freedom.

In the next chapter we'll discuss the basic principles of genuine forgiveness as experienced in the context of Theophostic Ministry.

SIX

Releasing Those Who Have Hurt Us

How Many Times Must I Forgive Someone?

In Matthew 18 Jesus teaches Peter and the other disciples about genuine forgiveness in response to Peter's question, "How many times do I need to forgive? Seven times?" (see v. 21). Jesus tells him, "I do not say to you, up to seven times, but up to seventy times seven." I can almost see Peter's shoulders slump at this point. I suspect that Peter asked Jesus this because he had forgiven someone many times, yet the person was not changing his behavior, and Peter was tired and hoping there was a forgiveness quota.

Jesus goes on to tell this story:

For this reason the kingdom of heaven may be compared to a certain king who wished to settle accounts with his slaves. And when he had begun to settle them, there was brought to him one who owed him ten thousand talents [about $20,000,000 in current U.S. funds]. But since he did not have the means to repay [remember, he was a servant on slave wages], his lord commanded him to be sold, along with his wife and children and all that he had, and repayment to be made. The slave therefore falling down, prostrated himself before him, saying, "Have patience with me, and I will repay you everything" [which was a lie, since he had no money]. And the lord of that slave felt compassion and released him and forgave him the debt. But that slave went out and found one of his fellow slaves who owed him a hundred denarii [about a day's wage]; and he seized him and began to choke him, saying, "Pay back what you owe." So his fellow slave fell down and began to entreat him, saying, "Have patience with me and I will repay you." He was unwilling however, but went and threw him in prison until he should pay back what was owed.

MATTHEW 18:23-30 (brackets mine)

The traditional interpretation of this passage is that Jesus is trying to teach His disciples about the great love God has for us and the forgiveness He offers all who come to Him to receive it. I believe this passage also teaches us some important truths about forgiveness and how we can find release from those who have hurt us.

Take an Account

Principle One: *Forgiveness requires we take an account.* "And when he had begun to settle them [the accounts of the servants], there was brought to him one who owed him ten thousand talents" (Mt 18:24).

The king called his servants to give an account of what was owed because we cannot forgive a debt we do not know exists or if we do not know what the amount is on the note. (Here again is an example of dealing with the specific reasons for offense.) Theophostic Ministry helps you to identify the specific reason for your pain by helping you follow the painful emotional trail back to the source of your emotional pain. Until you know what was done to you and the extent of the damage, you cannot forgive the offender.

People dissociate and repress their emotional pain in order to avoid feeling it all the time, but the pain has to be exposed before the true debt can be realized. All of us suppress bad feelings at times. This was one of my primary defenses against emotional pain as a child and for most of my adult life. If I felt bad about something I would just push the bad feelings down. By pushing the feelings down I was also suppressing the memory picture of the event itself. If you do this long enough, you will "forget" that the event even happened. The mind simply relocates the memory outside of your conscious reality.

Yet, if we want true freedom from our offender, we must access the memory of the offenses, so we can take an account of them. Some misinformed people suggest that painful repressed memories do not exist except where they have been implanted by a counselor or minister. The truth is, it is not the pictures of the memory that are repressed so much as the pain that those pictures surface.

A Debt Only Jesus Can Repay

Principle Two: *If we look to the offender for healing, restitution, or compensation we will only be more wounded. The one who has caused the pain does not have the means to repay the debt or remove the pain* *from our lives.* "He did not have the means to repay ..." (Mt 18:25).

The servant had a wife and children and was living on slave wages or less. He did not have the means to repay the $20,000,000 he owed the king. The king needed to know what the servant owed, but he also realized that the servant couldn't repay this enormous debt—in several lifetimes.

Often wounded people will look to their abuser for repayment. For example, when Tim came to me for ministry, he was a depressed and frustrated businessman. He described himself as a workaholic and very driven. I asked him to tell me about his relationship with his father, as there is often a correlation between emotionally driven men and their "Daddy wounds."

Many times a man's driven, workaholic behavior is the vain attempt of a suppressed little boy still looking to his father for approval and acceptance. The father's emotional absence in the boy's life created an insatiable wound that has never been filled. When the man was a little boy, he had a God-created need to receive love, acceptance, and approval from his father. This need went unmet, and the result was a wound that neither the wounder nor anyone else could ever fill. The same is true for those who marry looking for someone to meet their childhood needs that have become wounds. No one can address these wounds and take away the pain. The only remedy is God's healing.

Tim went on to describe a father who was distant and often gone. To that day Tim's father still would not respond with words of affirmation when Tim would call and report his business successes. At one moment in our conversation Tim said,

"No matter what I do, he never notices!" and began to weep. Tim was looking to one "who did not have the means to repay" for collection. This will never work.

Survivors of Satanic Ritual Abuse (SRA)[1] often feel a huge emotional void, and live in a constant cycle of defeat because the void can never be filled. Compassionate Christian ministers who try to fill these insatiable "love voids" will "burn out" trying to fill them, which, in turn, confirms what the occult programmer has instilled in the victim: "No one can ever really love you." The truth is, only Jesus can heal this wound. The debt is too great, and only He can "pay it back" and restore the losses of these lives. God promises: "And I will restore to you the years that the locust hath eaten, the cankerworm, and the caterpiller, and the palmerworm, my great army which I sent among you. And ye shall eat in plenty, and be satisfied, and praise the name of the Lord your God, that hath dealt wondrously with you: and my people shall never be ashamed" (Jl 2:25-26, KJV).

When we seek to find resolution or restitution from those who were responsible for our original wounding or look to others later in life to fill these vacuums we will always be disappointed. Only truth from the Holy Spirit, spoken softly and gently, can calm the raging waves of our painful past.

Anger Must Be Released

Principle Three: *Anger is a normal reaction to injustice but must be released before freedom will come.* "But since he did not have the means to repay, his lord commanded him to be sold, along with his wife and children and all that he had, and repayment to be made" (Mt 18:25).

When the king came to realize the severity of the situation, he reacted with anger. It looks like he may have even over-reacted a bit. Not only did he command the servant to be sold into slavery, he sent the wife and innocent children away with him. It appears that the king was good and stirred up, and rightfully so. The king's anger was actually a normal and healthy response to this servant's apparent irresponsible behavior. How this servant could have ever gotten so deeply in debt is difficult to comprehend. The king knew the money was gone and he was never going to get it back. All there was to do was become angry and rightly punish the servant.

The Christian community has little tolerance for anger as an emotion. We're told that anger is sin and that true spiritual people don't get angry. Many parents also teach their children not to express their anger. Yet the Bible tells us to "be angry, and yet do not sin" (Eph 4:26). "Sinless anger" sounds like an oxymoron. Anger becomes a sin when it is harbored and festers, or if it is acted out unrighteously. Paul describes how sinful anger originates in the last part of this verse when he says, "Don't let the sun go down on your anger or you will give the devil an opportunity."

Satan wants us to dwell on our anger day after day and do nothing about it. He wants us to turn the anger inward and bury it deeply. The reason for this is so that later, when something else happens that is remotely similar to the original offense, the demonic forces will take the "opportunity" to stir up this old anger so that we will react inappropriately and express more anger than the situation calls for. The problem with expressing old anger in a new situation is it never depletes the original anger. Until the anger is identified and then released by surrendering it to the Lord Jesus in the context of the original event (memory), we are destined to perpetually "dump" the old anger on whoever happens to trigger the original memory. It is not that we are just angry people. We are specifically angry in specific places for legitimate reasons. However, new events trigger this legitimate anger and it is illegitimately released in the new context. It is here that Satan has been given opportunity (see Eph 4:26).

Forgiveness Is Not Dependent on the Offender

Principle Four: *The integrity and sincerity of the indebted wounder is not critical for true forgiveness to be administered.* "The slave therefore falling down, prostrated himself before him, saying, 'Have patience with me, and I will repay you everything'" (Mt 18:26).

At first glance it seems the servant has come to his senses and is truly sorry for what he has done. However, something the servant says reveals his true heart even in that moment. When he promised, "I will pay back the full amount," he lied and revealed a heart of deceit. He knew that he could never repay his debt, and he had no intention of ever doing so. The fact that he had run up such an enormous debt tells us that he was a thief through irresponsible behavior.

Many times we want to offer forgiveness that's contingent on the attitude and integrity of the one we are forgiving. Yet genuine forgiveness has nothing to do with the condition of the one being forgiven. Forgiveness is not dependent on the person wanting or asking for it. Forgiveness is *aphiemy*, a cutting off, a release or sending away of the offense or debt. The king can cut off the debt, whether the servant wants it or has a change of heart or not.

Forgiveness is focused on the debt, not the debtor. When John the apostle wrote, "If we confess our sins, He is faithful and just to *forgive us our sins* and to cleanse us from all unrighteousness" (1 Jn 1:9, italics mine), the focus of forgiveness is on the sin, not the sinner. The sin receives the action of the verb *forgive*. God releases or cuts off the sin, not the sinner. Actually, to pray correctly, we ought to say, "God forgive my sin," not "forgive me." I do not want God to cut me off, but I do want Him to release me of my sin and debt.

Forgiveness Requires Compassion

Principle Five: *Genuine forgiveness requires that we find compassion.* "And the lord of that slave felt compassion and released him and forgave him the debt" (Mt 18:27).

If we try to forgive while we are still feeling the pain of the offense, forgiveness will be impossible. When we are able to follow our pain to its true source and find God's truth, the pain of the offense leaves. When the pain is gone it will be replaced with peace and a sense of compassion. The peace and compassion we feel enable us to truly release another's debt.

The king felt compassion, and this allowed him freely to release the servant of the debt. His compassion for the servant exposed the true heart of the king and his true belief system. Compassion is the benevolent action we take toward another as a result of our own healing, and the resulting emotional identification we are able to make with the one who has offended us. When we come into truth and receive God's grace and forgiveness, we can more clearly see the person who has hurt us from God's perspective. We are able to identify with the offender as a fellow sinner who is in need of truth, just as we are. I can forgive you when I see in you that which is also present in at least some measure in myself. I may not have ever sexually abused anyone, but I have offended others with my words and actions in other ways.

Apparently the Church of Rome had a noncompassionate, judging attitude toward others, which caused Paul to write, "you are without excuse, every man of you who passes judgment, for in that you judge another, you condemn yourself; for you who judge practice the same things" (Rom 2:1). These Roman Christians had not yet identified themselves in the lives of others. When we come into the truth God has for us and receive His perfect peace, we can experience the release of the need for revenge and the cutting off of the debt (forgiveness). When the king found compassion, he released the slave and forgave the debt.

Sharon and I had been married about ten years when the Lord blessed us with our first child. Sarah was a delightful child who had an effervescent personality that could win over anyone's heart. However, this blessing came to a tragic end when little Sarah developed an undetected brain hemorrhage. She survived three brain surgeries, but eventually lost her fight for life and the Lord took her home. Sharon and I entered into the darkest time of our lives as we grieved the loss of our little girl.

Before Sarah died, I had already begun to counsel people who would come to me with different issues and losses. Now and then someone would come who had suffered the loss of a loved one. I would say, "I know how you feel," and give other pat answers. The truth is, I did not know how they felt, because I had not experienced anything like what they were experiencing. I could offer sympathy but not compassion. Sympathy says, "I feel sorry for you." Compassion says, "I know the pain you carry, for I, too, have carried a similar burden."

Compassion can bear up the one in pain in a way that nothing else can. This is only possible because we can feel the pain. Many people tried to console me through my grief, and I appreciated it. However, when someone came and said, "I know what you feel; I, too, have experienced the death of a child," something inside of me reached out and grabbed hold of that person's words of encouragement. This person knew the pain of what I was feeling and could offer me true compassion.

The Scripture says, "The king felt compassion." I do not know what the king saw in the servant, because we know the servant wasn't sincere, but something struck the chords of compassion in the king's heart. "The king released him and forgave him his debt."

Forgiveness Offers Emotional Release

Principle Six: *Forgiveness emotionally releases the one offering the forgiveness, but may have no impact on the one whose debt is cleared.*

The king "released him and forgave him the debt. But that slave went out and found one of his fellow slaves who owed him a hundred denarii; and he seized him" (Mt 18:27-28).

Notice the two contrasting words in this verse: "released" and "seized." Here you see the true benefactor of forgiveness. When the king *released* the servant, he became free of the anger and the stresses of maintaining the note. The servant, on the other hand, was still in bondage to his evil heart, and *seized* his fellow worker.

Jesus wanted Peter to understand that forgiveness frees the forgiver. The fellow who caused trouble for Peter needed to be forgiven so that Peter could be free. Peter's concern was how long he would have to carry his resentment, frustration, and pain before he could cut this guy off and bury him, as the king had planned to do to the servant. Jesus suggested here that if Peter looked closely enough at this man, he might just find something with which he could identify. He might discover, like the lady I mentioned earlier, that his offender, like her abuser, was a lonely, hurting soul who was also deceived and wounded by lies that needed God's grace and mercy.

When we forgive someone, it doesn't mean that person will change his or her offensive behavior. Only God can change people, and He will do so only if they want to change. Of course, our forgiveness could have a positive impact on the offender and might motivate that person to seek change and renewal, but we have no guarantee this will happen.

Forgiveness has the power to change only the one forgiving, not the one being forgiven. The good news is that we can be emotionally free from other people and their behavior, whether they ever change or not. Other people's behavior does not have the power to control us emotionally. Of course, people do exert control over others in marriages and other relationships, but this is not true control. The one being controlled believes the lie that the other person has control over him or her. If we believe that we are powerless and weak (even though we are not), we will be rendered powerless by others' words and actions.

Battered wives are dominated by their husband's emotional control, and that's why they feel trapped. Of course, in some cases the husband physically holds the wife against her will, but most of the time the woman cannot be free because she does not believe she can be. The angry husband triggers her childhood lie-based thinking, causing her to feel the same powerlessness that she may have felt as a child in a similar abusive situation. As a child, she was helpless and powerless to do anything to change her world, but today she is an adult. The problem is that her childhood experiential feelings are more powerful than the logical truth of the present.

If Peter forgave his offender seven times seventy (490 times), he would still be in the same place as he started if he did not find freedom from the bondage he had with his offender. The number of times we forgive will have little or no impact on whether the person who has offended us will act differently in the future. When we forgive, we must do so without any expectation that the person being forgiven will change. We must let go of any expectation that the one who wounded us will or can repay the debt. Christ can release us from the pain of the wounder's indebtedness, as we are willing to let go and look to Him who can replace pain with perfect peace.

Forgiveness Is Not Reconciliation

Principle Seven: *Forgiveness should not be confused with reconciliation.* There is no indication that the king and the servant ever became friends, ate lunch together, or sat with each other in church. As a matter of fact, the Scripture says their relationship never got any better than it was the day the servant was called in to give an account. Yet the king truly released the servant and forgave him his debt.

Remember, forgiveness is focused on the debt, not the debtor. My banker could call me and inform me that he has made the decision to cancel all my debts. It really does not matter if I am happy, grateful, desirous, or even willing to receive. If he chooses to release me of the debt, I have no choice but to be released. I can scream, cuss, or protest loudly. I can tell him I will not accept it. I can even continue to send in my monthly payments, but the bottom line is, I owe the bank nothing if the banker decides to tear up my note.

The power to forgive lies totally in the hands of the one who holds the note. The one in debt has nothing to say about whether forgiveness occurs. Reconciliation, however, is a completely different matter, and the two shouldn't be confused. Forgiveness is letting go of the debts others owe you. Reconciliation is about relationship. I cannot have a relationship with someone who has hurt me, yet has never come clean with what he or she has done. Relationship requires transparency and integrity from both parties. I can forgive you (release you of your debt) whether you want me to or not, but I cannot be reconciled to you until you accept responsibility for your sin. Reconciliation requires the debtor to take full responsibility for his or her actions, confess the error of his or her way, and in penitent brokenness seek reconciliation from the one he or she has offended. At this time the one offended is in the position to receive God's grace to enter into relationship if he or she chooses.

However, if the debtor does not admit the wrong and accept full responsibility for his or her offense, reconciliation is not possible. Paul says, "If possible, *so far as it depends on you,* be at peace with all men" (Rom 12:18; emphasis mine). Reconciliation is based upon relationship. You cannot have relationship in the context where an offender refuses to do the right thing.

I used to believe recovery from abuse necessitated confronting one's abuser. I believed that as victims of abuse became more emotionally stable and strong, they would need to confront and hold their abusers accountable. Somehow I believed that doing this would empower them. I now see that this is not true or necessary. As people come into perfect peace, they are able to view their abusers through the eyes of Christ, with genuine compassion and forgiveness. It is here they find true freedom.

Sometimes the victim stills feels a need to confront, but it is done from a different posture than before. I used to encourage victims to connect with their "righteous anger" on the inside and use this as strength to face those who had hurt them. Today I neither encourage nor discourage confrontation. If the person feels a need to confront, I want to discern what is driving the need to do so. If it is anger, revenge, or any other negative emotion, I encourage the person to continue in healing until he or she can confront with perfect peace. When we confront from a place of peace rather than anger, the impact on the one accused of the abuse is incredible. There is much more power in confronting with peace than in doing so with anger.

The members of my sexual abuse survivors' group were some of the first recipients of Theophostic Ministry. Wanda was a young lady who had worked very hard for several years with me, and she was finally experiencing freedom as we used the Theophostic Ministry approach to healing. Wanda had been abused by her grandfather many times as a little girl. Before she underwent Theophostic Ministry, the very thought of confronting him caused her to feel small and powerless. We practiced the confrontation many times in group sessions through role-playing and talking to empty chairs, but Wanda made very little progress in this area.

As we began to use Theophostic Ministry, she became less and less fearful, and the feelings of powerlessness vanished as her lies were replaced with truth. She said that it was as if she was growing up on the inside with each healing moment. She reported feeling more and more like an adult, rather than feeling like a little child all the time. When she thought of the abusive memories, she felt strong and confident and had perfect peace.

Wanda called me at home one night a few days after finding release from her fears. She was very emotional when she first started speaking, and I thought she was having a crisis and needed help. It suddenly occurred to me, however, that she was excited, not upset. She told me, "Well, I did it!"

I had no idea what it was she had done, so I asked, "Did what?"

She went on to tell me that she had confronted her grandfather. Just by chance she had come face-to-face with him in the city park earlier that same day. When she saw him, she said she had expected to feel childlike, fearful, and overwhelmed. Instead, she felt no fear or panic, only calmness and confidence. She walked over to him and proceeded to confront him with what he had done to her. She did not feel angry, small, or fearful, and wasn't acting out of revenge. She was simply letting him know that the secret was out and that he was going to have to face it and its consequences.

After she finished telling him all she wanted to say, he denied it, but his response didn't bother her. She simply restated the facts with the same adultlike confidence. When he saw that she was not wavering, he began to panic and expressed fear of being put in jail and begged her not to tell anyone else. She told him that at this point she had forgiven him, and would leave the consequences of his crime to God and move on with her life. She also let him know that her forgiveness did not release him of being responsible for his actions in relation to God or those whom he had hurt.

Later on she did report his crimes to some members of the family she had suspected he had also hurt. Several of her cousins came forward with similar stories of their grandfather's abuse.

The change in Wanda's feelings and behavior clearly indicates her genuine healing and newfound freedom.

Prior to processing her memories and lies, she was still many months, maybe years, from confronting her grandfather. After a few sessions of Theophostic Ministry, she was ready and adequately prepared to do it.

Again, I am not suggesting that victims confront their abusers. This is between the person and God. Yet when genuine healing occurs, a change of perspective also occurs.

Victims see their abusers through the eyes of Christ, and they can do the impossible by forgiving their abusers with genuine heartfelt compassion. Jesus truly loves the vilest of sinners and desires for their complete redemption. When victims receive His eyes, they are released to love with His love.

What Will You Do With Your Pain?

You may have people in your life with whom you are angry, bitter, or resentful—and you probably have a right to feel this way. If they hurt you unjustly then they were wrong. Yet what are you going to do with this pain? You may believe that the anger protects you from further abuse or harm. This is not true. You may believe that if you forgive your abuser then he or she will be getting away with the crime. This also is not true. The anger, hate, and desire for revenge onto which you hold are stealing the good things that God has for you. He will go with you to the painful places in your mind and remove the deep hurt. He is willing to relieve you of all the anger and resentment, if you will allow Him to do so.

If you are in emotional bondage to someone who has hurt you, I encourage you to seek ministry from someone who understands the principles in this book and to go to Jesus with your pain. "Cast all your anxieties on him, for he [really] cares about you" (1 Pt 5:7, RSV).

SEVEN

Answers to Common Questions About Theophostic Ministry

People often ask me about Theophostic Ministry. This chapter addresses some of the more general questions people have about the basis of the ministry; it also seeks to dispel some of the false notions and misconceptions about Theophostic Ministry that have surfaced on the Internet.

Are the Theophostic Principles in the Bible?

A few critics of this ministry say that I have veered away from the traditional theological moorings of the faith, including repentance, discipleship, and the core issues of sin, and that my view of the nature of man (that is, the nature of the believer in Christ) and our ongoing sanctification is not completely in harmony with what is known as Reformed Theology. Some have written reviews that present unfounded conclusions and assumptions. Many of the negative reviews take my statements out of context and follow a format such as: "If Ed Smith said *that*, then he must mean *this* ..." It saddens me to read these reviews because I know that others are also reading them, and may believe they are factual and be steered away from this ministry and thereby forgo potential freedom.

I'm amazed that people can write papers and print conclusions and assumptions about what they think I believe and yet never talk with me about their concerns. Much of the information that appears on the Internet is quoted from those who criticize the ministry. None of these critics, as far as I know, have ever participated in a Theophostic Ministry session to personally witness God's healing grace. If they had and still sought to discredit this process, then they would also have to tell the "blind man" who has been healed to leave the temple.

Is Theophostic Ministry a biblically supported means of helping people to experience God? I suppose the first question to ask should be, "Is the word *theophostic* in the Bible?" The answer is no. That is, unless you break it down into its root word form of *theos,* which means God, and *phos,* which means light. Are the principles of Theophostic Ministry listed or discussed in the Bible? No, the writers of the Bible did not have these concepts from which to draw any more than they did any other scientific or medical framework. Just because the early church did not understand the concept of gravity did not mean that it did not exist. However, God did design and create the realities of the mind. The basic principles of Theophostic Ministry can be found in subtle forms throughout the Bible. They are evident in the way God has dealt with people throughout history.

Some say I have taken this Theophostic grid and have overlaid it onto Scriptures and am proof-texting the passages. The truth is, we all take some personal interpretation or grid to the Scriptures. It is impossible not to do so. However, I originally found this grid in Scripture, and it is from this grid that I continue to develop this process.

Theophostic Ministry is not a new concept. What God is doing through this ministry process is the same as He has done throughout the ages. He desires that we know the truth and walk in it. God uses daily situations, people, and life in general to test us, and expose us so that He might renew our thinking. Theophostic Ministry is about moving people to the place where they can receive truth at an experiential level. Theophostic Ministry is a systematized format by which this is more easily accomplished.

The Bible is full of examples of how God has operated within the principles taught in this approach to ministry. For example, we can see them operating in Peter's life when viewed through all four Gospel accounts, which I have included in summary in the following. The setting was the night that Jesus was to be betrayed. The Lord was telling His disciples about His coming arrest and death.

Jesus said to them, "You will all become deserters because of me this night; for it is written, 'I will strike the shepherd, and the sheep of the flock will be scattered!' But after I am raised up, I will go ahead of you to Galilee." Peter said to him, "Though all become deserters because of you, I will never desert you." Jesus said to him, "Truly I tell you, this very night, before the cock crows, you will deny me three times." Peter said to him, "Even though I must die with you, I will not deny you."

MATTHEW 26:31-35, NRSV

Jesus further said to Peter,

"Simon, Simon, listen! Satan has demanded to sift all of you like wheat, but I have prayed for you that your own faith may not fail; and you, when once you have turned back, strengthen your brothers." And [Peter] said to him,

"Lord, I am ready to go with you to prison and to death"

LUKE 22:31-33, NRSV

Jesus then led his disciples into the garden to pray. After he prayed, Judas came with a group of people to arrest Jesus. Then Simon Peter, who had a sword, drew it, struck the high priest's slave, and cut off his right ear. The slave's name was Malchus. Jesus said to Peter, "Put your sword back into its sheath. Am I not to drink the cup that the Father has given me?" (see Jn 18:1-11).

Then they seized him and led him away, bringing him into the high priest's house. But Peter was following at a distance. When they had kindled a fire in the middle of the courtyard and sat down together, Peter sat among them. Then a servant-girl, seeing him in the firelight, stared at him and said, "This man also was with him." But he denied it, saying, "Woman, I do not know him." A little later someone else, on seeing him, said, "You also are one of them." But Peter said, "Man, I am not!" Then about an hour later still another kept insisting, "Surely this man also was with him; for he is a Galilean." But Peter said, "Man, I do not know what you are talking about!" At that moment, while he was still speaking, the cock crowed. The Lord turned and looked at Peter. Then Peter remembered the word of the Lord, how he had said to him, "Before the cock crows today, you will deny me three times." And he went out and wept bitterly.

LUKE 22:54-62, NRSV

What followed was the Crucifixion, three days in the tomb, and then the Resurrection. Many days after the Resurrection, Jesus appeared to His disciples early one morning while they were out fishing. He called to them and they came to land and had breakfast with Him. After they had eaten, a discussion arose between Jesus and Peter.

When they had finished breakfast, Jesus said to Simon Peter, "Simon son of John, do you love me more than these?" He said to him, "Yes, Lord; you know that I love you." Jesus said to him, "Feed my lambs." A second time he said to him, "Simon son of John, do you love me?" He said to him, "Yes, Lord; you know that I love you." Jesus said to him, "Tend my sheep." He said to him the third time, "Simon son of John, do you love me?" Peter felt hurt because he said to him the third time, "Do you love me?" And he said to him, "Lord, you know everything; you know that I love you." Jesus said to him, "Feed my sheep. Very truly, I tell you, when you were younger, you used to fasten your own belt and to go wherever you wished. But when you grow old, you will stretch out your hands, and someone else will fasten a belt around you and take you where you do not wish to go." (He said this to indicate the kind of death by which he would glorify God.) After this he said to him, "Follow me." Peter turned and saw the disciple whom Jesus loved following them; he was the one who had reclined next to Jesus at the supper and had said, "Lord, who is it that is going to betray you?" When Peter saw him, he said to Jesus, "Lord, what about him?" Jesus said to him, "If it is my will that he remain until I come, what is that to you? Follow me!"

JOHN 21:15-22, NRSV

Let me explain how this passage reveals many of what I describe as Theophostic principles. *First, Jesus exposed Peter's lie-based thinking.* Jesus announced that He was about to be betrayed and killed and that all the disciples would soon scatter. Peter "boldly" spoke out, saying that he would die before he would deny Jesus. Jesus exposed him on the spot when He said, "before the cock crows three times you will deny me." Since we know that Peter would not be willing to die for Jesus, but instead would buckle in fear in just a few hours, we can safely say that Peter's proclamation was rooted in fear and not courage.

Peter's behavior is common to all of us. Something happens that triggers our lie-based thinking, which surfaces a negative emotion. Rather than coming clean with our feelings and our true thinking, we cover them over with a false presentation that puts us in a more positive light. Jesus' announcement of His forthcoming death triggered fear in Peter that he was unwilling to admit. Instead, he boasted of his commitment to die if necessary. Peter gave the right answer and the noble response (*logical truth*) but was not confessing his true feelings or his *experiential knowledge*. I believe Peter really wished that he could die if called to do so, and believed that this was the right thing to do, but his emotions did not match his logical data.

After Jesus prayed in the Garden of Gethsemane and the group came to arrest Him, Peter tried again to push through his fear when he cut off the man's ear. The Bible says that the disciples all fled as the soldiers arrested Jesus and led Him off to be tried.

Later we find Peter in the outer court while Jesus was being questioned. Here again Peter was trying his best to do the right thing. He was as close to the action as his fear would allow him. However, in the next few moments his fear was fully exposed. A woman at the gate questioned his connection to Jesus and Peter denied having been with Jesus. Then a little girl came up to him and identified him as one who had been with Jesus. This was as far as he could go with his performance based spirituality, as he began to swear and angrily deny the Lord. The Scriptures say that as the cock was crowing, Jesus looked over at him. The pain Peter must have felt when Jesus looked over at him in that moment must have surely been beyond comprehension.

Jesus was later crucified and placed in a tomb for three days, and then gloriously rose again. When He appeared to the disciples on the seashore it was to be His third appearance. I do not believe that Jesus did anything by chance. I believe that He intended to appear this third time to Peter in order to trigger the pain stored in Peter's mind concerning his denial of the Lord. It is also important to see how Jesus deliberately asked Peter three times if he loved Him. Even the Scriptures point this out when they say, "It hurt Peter to hear the Lord ask Him the *third* time." What was Jesus doing here? He was triggering and stirring up Peter's memory-based pain by way of association. (This technique is taught in the Theophostic Ministry Advanced Seminar.) Peter was now positioned to receive truth. It was in this moment of emotional pain that Jesus told Peter that he would indeed be willing to die for Him when he was old. Jesus said,

"Very truly, I tell you, when you were younger, you used
to fasten your own belt and to go wherever you wished.
But when you grow old, you will stretch out your hands,
and someone else will fasten a belt around you and take
you where you do not wish to go." (He said this to indicate the kind of death by which he would glorify God.)
After this he said to him, "Follow me."

JOHN 21:18-19, NRSV

Peter wanted to be willing to die for Jesus and was deeply
grieved that his fear had shut him down in the time of crisis.
However, Jesus told him that there would come a time when
he would pass the test and would lay down his life.

Prior to the denial of Christ, Peter spoke the correct answer
when he proclaimed that he would die for Jesus. That was a
good and right answer but it was just not what he really
believed experientially in that moment. He was actually scared
spitless and really did not know what else to say. Satan indeed
sifted him as wheat, just as Jesus said he would, and Peter came
up lacking when Satan exposed his true belief system, which
was based on fear. He acted on this fear and denied the Lord
three times.

I believe that when Peter heard the prophetic truth of his
own death, the fear that had led to his denial of the Lord was
erased from his mind. In the first few chapters of Acts we find
Peter standing in front of an enormous crowd in the same city
in which he denied Jesus and proclaiming Christ as His Messiah,
and over three thousand people were saved on that day.

The Bible is full of stories just like this. God has not
changed His methods. He still allows us to be exposed, to fall

apart emotionally, and to make poor choices so that we will be motivated to seek Him in order to know truth. Jesus is still willing to speak to us in our pain and to provide His peace, if we will listen.

Theophostic Ministry is simply the process of renewing the mind. Everything that we possess in our minds that needs to be renewed is stored in memory. Theophostic Ministry is about accessing memory, discerning the belief system held in the memory, and seeking to allow the Spirit of Christ to replace the falsehood in the memory with His truth.

Does Ed Smith believe that he has received a divine revelation from God with this process he has called Theophostic Ministry?
This idea first surfaced from a fellow out in California who feels called to discredit this ministry as well as several other noted ministries, including Dr. James Dobson and Focus on the Family. He has written a little booklet about Theophostic Ministry and claims that I believe I have received a divine revelation from God. When I first read this, I was humored by how ridiculous his claims were. However, some people who do not know him or me have assumed that because he has a web site he must be an authority.

For the record, I do not believe that I have received any revelatory information from God, nor have I ever made such a claim.[1] In the Basic Seminar manual where I have been said to have claimed such revelation I am merely saying that I had new insight into the Scripture that I had not had before. This is the same sort of statement a pastor might make as he addresses his congregation with a statement such as, "This morning I want to share with you what I believe is God's message for today." In this situation no one would think he was saying that he had had a new revelation; rather, they would understand this to refer merely to insight into the Word. We do not need new revelation. I believe that the Scripture is complete and all we need. I believe that "all Scripture is given by inspiration of God, and is profitable for doctrine, for reproof, for correction, for instruction in righteousness, that the man of God may be complete, thoroughly equipped for every good work" (2 Tm 3:16-17, NKJV). We receive hundreds of cards and letters from people all around the world who have received some measure of healing from Theophostic Ministry and who have also read the negative claims on the Internet. What is happening is that the people making the negative statements are actually discrediting themselves by what they have written, as recipients of Theophostic Ministry are experiencing genuine healing.

Does Theophostic Ministry teach that God is speaking new revelation to people during their sessions that supersedes or is equal in status to the Scriptures?

Again, when people report hearing, receiving, or seeing some truth in their memory, they are *not* receiving new revelation. The Holy Spirit is giving them specific applications of biblical truth for their memory situation. This is really no different than when someone says, "I was at work today and sensed the Lord wanted me to talk to my associate about his need for Christ." Did that person hear a word from God? I believe so. Was it extrabiblical? No, Scripture tells us, "Go therefore and make disciples ..." (Mt 28:19). What is received in a ministry session will never contradict, replace, or supersede the Word of God. If it does, then it is a falsehood and does not meet the test of Theophostic Ministry.

Theophostic Ministry is not a way to "get an inside word" from God. I once heard of a group of people who gathered together around a woman who was suffering from a dissociative disorder. They believed she had a "direct line" to God during her ministry sessions. They would have her ask God for direction for their own personal issues and lives. She would then "channel" the message from "God" back to them. She would also "prophesy" special words and messages from "God." *This is not Theophostic Ministry!* This looks much like divination and witchcraft. Stay clear of all forms of this practice.

Does Theophostic Ministry use guided imagery, directed visualization, or some form of hypnosis?

A few misinformed people on the Internet have made this claim, which is false. These people have never contacted this ministry to get the facts, and instead they have interpreted the printed materials from their own preconceived notions. For the record, *Theophostic Ministry unequivocally denounces all forms of guided imagery, minister/counselor directed visualization, and hypnosis.*

Some people report having visual images during the ministry session, and it is without question that visual pictures do play a part in a Theophostic session for *some* people. However, I believe that truth that comes in the form of mental pictures is simply one way that the Holy Spirit has chosen to reveal His truth to certain people. However, these pictures should never be the creation of the one administering the process. Anything in the mind of the person receiving ministry that is created by the minister is not Theophostic Ministry but rather visualization or guided imagery created by the minister or counselor.

Is there any danger that the one administering Theophostic Ministry might implant false information in a person's mind during a ministry session?
Theophostic Ministry is, in its most basic form, simply prayer. When we pray we enter into a meditative mode of spiritual receptivity, focusing on what God has for us.

In this prayerful state people are encouraged to follow the painful emotions that are surfaced to their original place in memory. Theophostic Ministry works only with memories that the people being ministered to come up with on their own, without the help, suggestions, or insinuations of the one doing ministry. The minister should never suggest anything concerning the content of the person's memory during the process, no matter how convinced he or she may be of its validity. Theophostic Ministry teaches the minister to get out of the way and refrain from all forms of suggestion or insinuation. The minister should ask only questions that reflect the information that the person has already revealed. A minister should *never* say things like, "I wonder if someone molested you?" or "You have symptoms of being molested as a child," or "I think you may be SRA, or a survivor of a government mind control project, or hold a high-ranking position in the Illuminati." Such statements are completely misleading, are forbidden, are out of line, and do not represent Theophostic Ministry in any form.

Theophostic Ministry does not lead a person to get into a relaxed or trance state any more so than any other typical ministry or counseling session. The person simply sits in a chair while focusing on his or her present negative feelings.

Theophostic Ministry avoids the use of hypnotic practices in any form. The minister does not have the person count backward, think of a safe place, or follow a swinging pocket watch. The minister simply asks the person to discern what he or she feels and why.

When the person identifies an emotion, the minister asks the person to allow the Spirit of Christ to help him or her to find any memory that contains the same or similar feelings. Some have accused Theophostic Ministry of implanting information because at times repressed memories do surface in a session. The people making these accusations do not believe that a person can forget a traumatic event, yet research has clearly demonstrated that memories can be repressed, and often are. Many children who are abused repress the memory as a way of surviving the abuse, and they may have no memory of the abuse, even as an adult. I have worked with women who surfaced horrific memories of sadistic sexual abuse. If their stories were true, I knew there would have to be internal scarring on the inside of their vaginal cavities, so I sent each of them to a medical doctor. Lo and behold, he found scar tissue that he attributed to abuse. So much for the denial of repressed memories.

All of us have aspects of our lives held in memories we cannot consciously access. Who remembers every aspect of his or her life? We remember parts and places, but only selected events are actually consciously available at any given time. The mind does not actually forget anything. It just stores things in places that we are not able to consciously access at will. Every aspect of our life's journey is carefully filed away somewhere in the mind.

I am notorious for losing things. I lose my keys, my glasses, and sometimes my car in the parking lot. As a matter of fact, as I write this paragraph I have lost a part of this computer (an extra hard drive) that I need but have no idea (consciously) where I have placed it. Yet the truth is, the hard drive is not really lost; my mind contains the information I need to find it. I just cannot access this information. As soon as I find the lost item, however, I will respond with something like, "Oh, yeah, that's where I left it." When I find the item, I will remember having placed it in that spot in the first place. It would be really nice if I could just command this information to surface, but I cannot. It has been stored outside of my conscious awareness.

In the same way, if something happens to me as a child that I do not want to remember, my mind can place the undesirable information in a place where I cannot consciously find it. This is a survival tactic. When my subconscious mind believes it is safe to release the information (as in a Theophostic session) it very well may release the traumatic memory.

How do we know what people are reporting are true memories?
I minister to people who are in obvious pain. When they come to me for ministry, they have many symptoms that clearly indicate something is wrong. They do not come reporting that life is great, that they are happy, and that all is well. I see people who are depressed, discouraged, self-loathing, angry, bitter, compulsive, self-mutilating, addicted, and sometimes dissociated. Along with all manner of emotional pain, they often exhibit a variety of physical conditions that match their emotional maladies. I believe that these people have become this way as either a consequence of sinful choices or as a response to what has happened to them in life and because of their interpretation about what happened. Theophostic Ministry is

a self-discovery process seeking to uncover the true source of our emotional pain. In this process people sometimes end up in memories of which they were consciously unaware. Repression had afforded them the ability to function without having to consciously live in the trauma reality.

Theophostic Ministry assumes that the memory is a compilation of impressions, interpretations, and recollections in the person's mind. It's critical to discern what experiential belief is producing the emotional pain in the person's life.

It is possible that a person might believe something happened that didn't, or that happened differently than the memory portrays it. For example, a man might surface a memory of being abandoned by his mother and left with relatives to be raised. He may believe his mother left him because she hated him and didn't want him, yet in reality the mother's heart may have broken when she had to let her child go due to forces beyond her ability to control. However, this is beside the point when it comes to the man's healing. If he believes the lie that he was not wanted, then this wound needs to be healed. What we remember is our reality, and it is in this reality that healing must occur. However, while we may have misrecorded some of the finer details in a memory, the substance and essence of what happened is usually highly acccurate.

Furthermore, a memory isn't invalidated simply because I do not have all the facts. I may not have all the data in the correct order, or all the dates lined up perfectly, for if I was hurt then I was hurt. People are in pain because they were hurt. Ministry begins with the pain, assuming that there was a real life hurt. If we can get all the facts straight this is good, but it is not essential for healing.

Can suggestible people make their way into a counselor's

office and passively open up their minds while the counselor plants thoughts into them, creating false memories? Perhaps, although I think this must be very rare, if even possible. To assume this is common is to discredit all the good ministers and counselors in our country who work with people who surface painful repressed events and to invalidate the hundreds of thousands of people reporting trauma. I also find it hard to fathom that people could believe a story to the extent that they would abreact in emotional pain and lose their ability to function in daily life. Real pain has real-life sources. A false memory is just that—it is false. A false memory cannot produce traumatic pain.

The number of people who are reported to have had false memory is miniscule compared to the enormous numbers of people reporting trauma that has surfaced in ministry sessions and who believe their trauma to be true. If a person is making up a story for whatever reason, then the person hasn't had a false memory—the story isn't a memory. If a person has a memory that contains inaccurate information, this does not make the memory false; it simply means it's a memory with inaccurate information.

While it's important to discover the truth of what happened at some point, the lies producing the pain in the memory should be addressed first. I work in the reality of the people with whom I am ministering. To project my reality or my belief about their realities will have little effect in releasing them from their pain. This is especially true as I work with victims of the occult. These people have suffered the most horrible atrocities one can imagine. Do I believe every detail of their experiences? No. Do I try to talk them out of their beliefs about such experiences? Never. I simply work in their reality and invite Christ to reveal His truth in the same.

Memory is not a pure science, but the lies found in people's memories can be discerned with clarity, for the most part. Does this uncertainty invalidate people's reports of being abused or traumatized? Not at all. For the most part I have no problem believing the essence of the stories that I hear. I just realize that every detail may not be totally accurate. When someone comes to me with traumatic emotional pain, something traumatic is likely at its source. I assume that this something occurred in the context of real-life experience. I do not assume that the person will have a perfect recollection of what occurred, but I hope to find enough evidence to establish what is believed in this experiential context. I look for the source of the pain (which of course is not the memory itself but the lie in the memory).

What convinces me more than anything else of the reality of repressed memory are the people I see who have been in pain all their lives who come into *the perfect peace of Christ* after having embraced the content of their repressed memories and having received truth from the Spirit of Christ. Many have done everything else available to alleviate their pain through traditional counseling, but only when they embrace their repressed memories and receive a freeing truth from God do they find peace.

The bottom line is, memory is stored experience. I might be able to create a false picture in a client's mind, but I cannot create a debilitating emotion arising from this false picture. Real pain is not a figment of one's imagination. Real pain has a real source.[2]

Does Jesus actually appear to people in their memories?
I do not think that Jesus Himself is appearing to people in their memories. The Scripture says, "[Jesus] alone possesses immortality and dwells in unapproachable light; whom no man has seen or can see" (1 Tm 6:16). The next time anyone will truly see Jesus is when He returns in the clouds. Furthermore, people doing genuine Theophostic Ministry do not ask questions such as "Do you see Jesus?" or make suggestions such as "Look for Jesus." These kinds of directives would be guiding and creating imagery. This is *not* Theophostic Ministry.

However, I think it's possible that people can see a visual representation of Jesus in their memories. I would call this visual a word picture or visual communication between the person and God. I have seen hundreds of people come into perfect peace after encountering truth in a visual form during a Theophostic session.

Is Theophostic Ministry New Age or any other secular form of helping people?
Theophostic Ministry is not based on any New Age concept or belief. It is totally Christ centered and Holy Spirit directed. Theophostic Ministry rests on the biblical principles of God's Word and on a basic understanding of what is known scientifically about how the mind works.

The same skeptics who attack this ministry for using scientific findings about how the mind works have no problem going to a medical doctor for help with a heart problem. It is the same science, just focused on a different part of the body. I do not endorse everything that is coming down the science pike, but there is an enormous amount of information available that has proven invaluable in increasing our effectiveness in mind renewal and ministry. God has given us minds to develop, and I believe that using the results of good research is being a good steward of what God has given us. Theophostic Ministry is being successfully used by thousands of churches and ministries all around the world who have found it to be biblically convivent and Jesus centered.

Does Theophostic Ministry replace the need for biblical instruction?

Not at all! In order to move toward maturity and completeness, every Christian needs discipleship, teaching, preaching, and instruction. Yet I believe we have become unbalanced. We have, for the most part, become a cognitive church, seeking to know God with our minds but not with our experience. I don't believe, as some do, that if our relationship with God is hindered that it is *always* because of sinful behavior or because we still have "sinful hearts." Believers often struggle in their relationship with God, not only because of unconfessed sin in their lives, but also because they believe things that are not true (lie-based thinking) and, as a consequence, live lives of defeat and relational breakdown with God. If I have been made right and have peace with God through the Lord Jesus Christ (see Rom 5:1) then my relationship is already in good standing, whether I feel like it is or not. If "there is ... no condemnation for those who are in Christ" (Rom 8:1) then I am not condemned, even if I feel that I am. Many Christians live as sin-free a life as possible; yet have minimal relational experiences with God. To have an experiential relationship with God, we have to come to know Him relationally in the same way that we know our spouse or other loved ones. I do not know my wife because I have studied about her or read books about her. I know her because I live with her and experience her daily.

In his final discourse to the church, Jesus commanded His disciples to go into the entire world with the gospel and to teach them all things that He had taught them (see Mt 28:19-20). The epistles instruct us to learn, grow in knowledge, and mature in our understanding. Discipleship and study of God's Word play an important part in this process. Theophostic Ministry is not about discipleship but rather about receiving a specific truth for the displacement of a specific lie. True healing releases us of our lie-based thinking so that we might be able to more effectively appropriate that which we logically hold to already as truth yet lack supportive experience for. This is not a case of either one or the other. We need to absorb the Word of God and be saturated in it, but we also need to experience the presence of Christ so that we might appropriate what we have cognitively received.

We are healed of our specific lies in a "Theophostic moment," but it is through teaching, discipleship, and living life that we come into maturity in Christ. Paul declares this when he says, "we proclaim Him, admonishing every man and teaching every man with all wisdom, that we may present every man complete in Christ" (Col 1:28).

Following this passage, Paul says, "let the word of Christ richly dwell within you, with all wisdom teaching" (Col 3:16). Here he indicates that we are not only to study the Word, but let it richly dwell within us; let it saturate us. He told Timothy to "give attention to the public reading of Scripture, to exhortation and teaching" (1 Tm 4:13). Scripture very clearly says that we need to study, learn, teach, and grow. Theophostic Ministry does not replace this admonition to study the Word of God; it merely opens the way for our study to be more effective.

We grow in our understanding and experience of the Lord as each life situation occurs. So a Christian who is faithful and seeks the face of God will grow and mature in Christ, whether he or she ever learns of Theophostic Ministry. When we cry out to God, He shows Himself strong. It is in this experience that we shed the lies that have hindered our walk. The writer of Hebrews said we must "lay aside every encumbrance [that which weighs us down; lies?] and the sin which so easily entangles us ... fixing our eyes on Jesus, the author and perfecter of faith" (Heb 12:1-2, commentary mine).

People often tell me, "Theophostic Ministry is not new." They then say, "This happened to me years ago during a crisis in my life when..." They describe how their emotional pain flared up, they cried out to God, and the Lord brought truth that released them of all their pain.

In our churches, we often teach people biblical knowledge without considering that they also need release from the lies that bind them. It might be better if we released them and then taught them, but at least we should do both, whichever the order may be. More information is no guarantee that people will walk in freedom. Logical truth will have difficulty overriding the power of experiential knowledge. We need experiential truth from the living Lord Jesus. Let me explain. If I am in bondage to the lie of fear in a traumatic memory, I will not likely be able to embrace the logical truth that "perfect love casts out fear" (1 Jn 4:18). However, when I go to the memory and embrace the fear and the lie, I am in the position to hear the specific personalized truth from the experiential presence of Jesus. When this occurs, I am then able to embrace the logical truth from the Word of God.

It requires a new experience to change or override lies learned through an old experience. If my childhood experiences have taught me that I am worthless and no good, cognitively teaching me otherwise as an adult will have little impact. You can have me memorize verses that declare that I am the righteousness of God, fully acceptable though Christ, holy and perfected in Him, and I may still walk in defeat until my experiential lies are displaced with experiential divinely provided truth. Until then, my experience will usually override my logic—unless I am able to muster up strong discipline and determination. I need an experience with Jesus that dispels these lies so that I can appropriate these logical truths and enter into maintenance-free victory.

Isn't Theophostic Ministry just another form of deliverance ministry?

Theophostic Ministry is a mind-renewal ministry, *not* a deliverance ministry, and it does not see demons as the problem, or exorcism as the final solution. Deliverance from demons is not the answer to people's emotional pain. I do believe many people are demonized, but I also know that these same demons can be sent away without any fight or resistance at the appropriate time, once the lies in these people's memories are replaced with truth. This is not to say that you will not encounter demons when using Theophostic Ministry, or that demons are not having influence on those they inhabit.

I have spent thousands of hours with demonized people over the years, and have encountered hundreds of fully manifested demonic experiences. I have run the full gamut in "spiritual warfare," from fighting and screaming at demons in an effort to "wear them down" until they "let go" to now giving a direct and clear command that they immediately obey. I know my place in Christ and simply expect the demon to immediately do what it is told, and this is my common experience now.

What we say we believe about Satan and demons and warfare actually contrasts with what we often practice. We believe that Jesus defeated Satan on the cross and that we are totally victorious in Him. We believe that we have been given all authority (see Eph 1:22), that we are "more than conquerors" (Rom 8:37, NKJV), and that we "overcame him because of the blood of the Lamb and because of the word of their testimony" (Rv 12:11). Yet, we still choose to engage the demons in warfare. Most spiritual warfare books tell us that the devil is defeated, but then proceed to instruct us on how to battle a defeated foe. This really makes no sense. How can we be victorious and "more than conquerors" and yet have to fight? If I have won the game, why do I have to go into overtime? The battle is truly over and there is no more warfare to be had. Satan already knows this, but he is happy to oblige us in "wrestling" needlessly. Our unnecessary battling is a nostalgic reminder of the kingdom status he once held.

It is very easy to become distracted in an "unnecessary" battle and lose sight of our calling. Some assume the battle is necessary, since this is what they are doing. Just because we are doing something does not make it a necessity, however. I used to battle demons, too, but not anymore. Demons always do exactly what they are commanded to do. They are defeated and under our authority. When a demon does not comply with our directions, then it is either not a demon (which can be the case in dissociative disorders) or else we are unsure of our authority position.

For it was "through death He might render powerless him who had the power of death, that is, the devil; and might deliver those who through fear of death were subject to slavery all their lives" (Heb 2:14-15). If he has been rendered *powerless,* how much power does he have?

Does Theophostic Ministry take a soft position on sin and make the sinner out to be a poor victim of his or her circumstances? To answer this question I've adapted the following material from the Basic Seminar manual.

Sometimes the pain people carry is not the result of having been unjustly wounded, but is coming from a self-inflicted wound or sin. In these times, people suffer emotional pain due to their own choice rather than as a result of what someone else has done to them. I am referring to willful acts of sin.

When I use the word sin, I am referring to any behavior we engage in as a result of choices that we make which are less than God's ideal desire for our lives. These sinful choices are often vain attempts to relieve us of emotional pain or by acting this pain out in a sinful manner. For example, I might act out my pain by defending myself with harsh words if someone triggered my lies of inadequacy. I might try to comfort myself for feeling worthless by eating food even though I am not hungry.

The word for sin most often used in the New Testament is the Greek word *harmatia,* which means, in its basic understanding, to miss the mark. When we seek to heal ourselves, we "miss the mark" and never know the full restoration God intends for us. Sin may also be the initial response we have carried of anger or hate toward the one who wounded us. This reaction was predictable and righteous when the event occurred (see Eph 4:26), but this same anger is destructive and deceiving for us who continue to carry it (see Eph 4:31). Many who have been wounded believe the anger they hold benefits them and empowers them. The opposite is true. This "reactionary anger" must be dealt with and forsaken if they are ever to know complete release.

Some have suggested that to overcome sin we simply need to confess it, turn from it, and choose to obey God. This is a traditional view but is it really any different than keeping the Law and works salvation? Many people are in this cycle of defeat and see no way free.

This approach has, at its foundation, overcoming sin as the solution. It has also forgotten that the only cure for sin is the cross. It is implied that if we overcome sin (which we cannot do), we would walk in victory. I want to suggest that if we focus on sin as the only problem and do not address the lies behind the sin, we set ourselves up for ultimate defeat and a cycle of perpetual confession, repentance, and performance-based spirituality. Though this is a common practice in the church, it has afforded limited success except from the ones most disciplined. Sin is always precluded by a thought. This thought is based on a deception at some level. The lie is present in every sinful choice and act we make. If the lie is not identified and removed, the sin will perpetually and predictably resurface when the pain is triggered.

Some would suggest that sin is rooted in the heart of the true Christian just as in the lost person. It is then from the sinful heart that the thought emerges which results in behavior. If this is true then there is no hope of present victory. If my heart is evil and sin-filled then the cross did not make me new; I will perpetually sin in a never-ending cycle. However, if my heart is made new in Christ Jesus, then as my mind is renewed I can live out my "holy and blameless" state before God.

I believe that the heart of the true believer in Christ, those who are "partakers of the divine nature" (2 Pt 1:4), is the temple and dwelling place of the Spirit of God. If we are new creatures in Christ then we have put off the "old self" and have put on the "new self," which is righteous and born of God. The heart that was wicked and evil has now become "holy and blameless before Him" (Eph 1:4). What was a kingdom of darkness and the throne of Satan has become the very home and temple of a Holy God! Can a holy God dwell in a heart that is not holy and pure? However, "if any man is in Christ, he is a new creature" (2 Cor 5:17) and his heart is a heart of righteousness and God is perfectly happy to live there.

If you hold a different theological view from me, this is all right. I will never agree with all of you nor will all of you ever agree with me. I simply encourage you to *not* throw out the "Theophostic" baby with the "theological" bathwater.

The truth is, we have to think before we act out sinfully. I am suggesting that if we can find freedom from the lies we experientially believe, we are less likely to think sinfully and therefore less prone to sin. I have lie-based thinking that gets triggered; this stirs up a bad feeling; I have to decide to either express the pain, cover the pain, or go to the source of the pain (Theophostic Ministry). If I do not go to the source and find truth, I must then make a choice as to whether I will act it out or not.

As I mentioned in an earlier chapter, according to James 1:14-15 the sin process flows in a predictable fashion. First, the enemy provides a temptation or life situation, which is tailored to trigger an original thought or experiential lie. The experiential lie is a belief, which was received during the life experience. We may or may not consciously think the original lie/thought in our current situation, but nevertheless it is aroused. For example, if we are raised in an alcoholic home, we might learn a belief such as, "Life is out of control and I am responsible to do something to remove the chaos." Once the original thought is triggered and stirred, a matching emotion will emerge. Now we feel out of control. The enemy then provides a workable solution to deal with the "feelings" of being out of control. He might suggest we go to the refrigerator and binge, read a pornographic magazine, clean the house, yell at the kids, jog around the block, go to church, etc. We now act on the enemy's solution and the painful, anxious, or fearful emotions are masked until the original lie is triggered again. In the meantime we may feel guilty for the choice we have made, so we confess our sin and repent and promise not to do it again. We may be successful for a time, but at some point the lie and its emotion will find their way back through our behavior.

Often victory is falsely equated with the cessation of a particular behavior and its replacement with a more acceptable one. For example, we may stop compulsive eating or not eating by replacing it with daily jogging (as is often the case with anorexia). We might quit drinking and overcompensate with religious behavior. Any attempt to overcome our lie-based pain by adjusting our behavior is works salvation. The lie still remains and the emotions driving the compulsion are merely routed through a different avenue.

I am not belittling the power and the destructive reality of sin in one's life. Sinful behavior must be contended with, but if overcoming it becomes the focus for finding victory, defeat is inevitable since the only cure for sin is the cross of Christ.

Due to the poor success rate of overcoming sin, Christians have developed other approaches for dealing with sin. One approach is to become more tolerant with sin and less judgmental. Someone once said, "If you first do not succeed simply lower your standard." The church no longer takes a hard line with sin as it did in former times, primarily because of the low success rate in overcoming it. These days it seems the local church is more concerned with keeping everyone happy, meeting perceived needs, growing numbers, and building buildings. Today, a pastor could risk losing his job should he become too straightforward in confronting the sins of his congregation, but is applauded for building a family life center.

We have even created a new terminology for sin. What used to be called adultery is now only having an affair. What used to be called fornication became premarital sex (which says nothing about the morality of the act, just the point in time at which it occurred). What the Bible calls fornication (sex before marriage) now has a positive ring to it. We refer to our children's immoral behavior (fornication) as their being "sexually active." This almost sounds like something healthy and normal. What the Bible clearly describes as a perversion and an abomination is now just having an alternative sexual preference (see Rom 1:19-27).

It doesn't matter how you dress sin up, redefine it, or package it, its outcome still results in separation and death. Please do not be deceived as Eve was with the Serpent's argument, "You will not surely die" (Gn 3:4, NKJV). The death, which results from sin, is worse than physically dying; it is a death of one's spiritual connectedness with God. Sin has separated the unbeliever from the true life source (God), as a branch cut off from the tree. The limb may appear to be alive, separated from the trunk of the tree, but ultimately it withers and dries up and dies. However, I believe when people come to know Christ and become a partaker of the divine nature, they are eternally sealed. Willful and unconfessed sin no longer impacts our eternal destination, but it does hinder the ongoing fellowship God so desires for His beloved (see 1 Jn 1:9-10).

God's laws are consistent. If the "wages of sin is death" (Rom 6:23), it does not matter that you do not feel guilty or if your therapist tells you otherwise; death (or separation from God) is still the consequence. We, as a country, have worked hard at rewriting the laws of God to better suit our particular lifestyles, but the consequences of disobeying the original remain the same. If the road sign says, "Do not enter! Deep drop-off ahead! Hazardous to your health!" and you disobey and drive off the end of the road, you will crash on the rocks below. For some people this law may be too restricting and a violation of their personal rights. They may decide to change the sign to say, "Drive wherever you desire and practice safe driving. Wear your seat belts." The problem is, should they proceed down the road past the warning sign, they will still wind up on the rocks and be just as dead. The law can be rewritten but the consequences remain constant. When we sin, we suffer and die. No kind of ministry or amount of sessions will relieve a soul of its pain when the root is unconfessed sin. Sin's only cure is the cross of Jesus: "without shedding of blood there is no forgiveness" (Heb 9:22).[3]

The driving motivation to put off the sins in my life was for too long to become something: more holy, more righteous, less sinful, more like Jesus. Today I do not put off sinfulness so that I might become something that I am yet to be but rather because I am something. I am a saint (hagios = holy), the righteousness of God (2 Cor 5:21), holy and beloved, chosen of God (Col 3:12), child of light (Eph 5:8), blameless (Eph 1:4), accepted, complete and the fullness of Christ (Eph 1:23), a new creation (2 Cor 5:17) and more in Christ. I put off sinful behavior because it is not fitting for me to behave in a manner contrary to the new nature I have been given (2 Pt 1:4), I am a new man and my old man is dead (Rom 6:6). For I have been "raised with Christ," (so now I can) seek those things which are above, where Christ is, sitting at the right hand of God (where I am also (Eph 2:6). (Therefore I can) ...set [my] mind on things above, not on things on the earth. For [I have] died, and [my] life is hidden with Christ in God (Col 3:1-3, adapted).

Will Theophostic Ministry work with a person who does not know Christ?

There are many people now in the kingdom of God because they found peace in their minds though the administering of Theophostic Ministry and then were introduced to their Healer. When the nonbeliever finds healing grace from God, he or she very well may become highly motivated to move into an eternal relationship with God through faith. This happened often in the Gospels. Jesus did not require a life commitment from those He healed. Yet many came to be His followers and worshiped Him, once they received His healing. The blind man did not even know who Jesus was until after he received his sight and was thrown out of the temple. Later he discovered Jesus' identity and worshiped Him.

Some have mistakenly believed the notion that God will not hear or speak to a nonbeliever in Christ. If this is true, then why did God in the flesh (Jesus) find it easy to have fellowship and converse with the sinner? Jesus was very comfortable in conversing and ministering to the sinners and nonbelievers of His day. The truth is, Jesus had a hard time communicating and having fellowship with the so-called righteous in the Gospel stories.

Just a few weeks ago a lady came to my house to discuss some business issues. She was not a believer. After our business matters were settled I asked her how she was doing in her personal life. She reported that she was having a difficult time in her life. I asked a few more questions and she began to open up to me and deep pain began to surface. I shared with her the basic Theophostic principles and then asked her if she would like to be free of this pain. She said she would.

I did not talk about Jesus, the church, her need for salvation, or the apparent sin in her life. I simply invited her to feel the emotions that she was feeling. A painful childhood memory surfaced. We identified the reason for the pain (the lies she believed) and I asked her to simply report whatever she saw, sensed, or heard as I asked the Lord to reveal His truth to her. After a few moments she responded with truths that had come into her thinking. I asked her to try to find the pain that was present when we started the process. She reported that it was all gone and that she felt "real good" (that translates into perfect peace). I asked her where the truth that she had received had come from. She said it was from God. I asked her if she would like to have the same peace in her heart that she was feeling in her mind, and she was eager to receive the Lord Jesus.

It is important to note that mind renewal does not constitute salvation. A person can have renewing of the mind and still be eternally separated from God. I have seen many people come to a saving knowledge of the Lord Jesus by offering them His healing grace before I try to talk to them about their eternal destiny. I simply begin where the person is—in pain. This is the same place Jesus often started when ministering to people. As people find peace in their minds, the possibility of peace in their hearts becomes very appealing.

Is it possible that my life will become more painful if I open up the hidden places of pain in my memories?
Some have suggested that people who receive this form of ministry actually get worse before they get better. This is sometimes the truth. It is not because Theophostic Ministry causes more pain. It is because the person's emotional pain has been repressed and the painful emotions are now being released. This was true for me. I did not know that I was carrying repressed anger and rage due to hundreds of childhood experiences where I was not permitted to be angry. It was not until I began to allow the Holy Spirit to take me to these hidden places that my rage and anger surfaced. Up until this time I had actually been proud that I had always controlled my anger. I saw this controlled behavior as spiritual prowess, when in fact it was a childhood defense against pain. I am excited to say that after many healing sessions I have far less anger to surface. Even though I felt worse before I felt better, I am thoroughly enjoying the peace on this side of the journey.

If you are carrying pain that you are hesitant to uncover for fear that it will get worse before it gets better, remember that it is Jesus who awaits you on the other side with His perfect peace. It is also Jesus who will walk with you every step along the way. "Be anxious for nothing, but in everything by prayer and supplication with thanksgiving let your requests be made known to God. And the peace of God, which surpasses all comprehension shall guard your hearts and your minds in Christ Jesus" (Phil 4:6-7).

EIGHT

What to Expect in a Session

Be Discerning

Ironically, an unfair rule exists that says a ministry will be judged not by what it teaches or its founding principles, but rather by the results of those least capable or qualified to perform the ministry. In other words, even though tens of thousands have proven Theophostic Ministry to be a highly effective ministry tool to bring about lasting healing and change in people, it is often defined by the reports of the "nightmare sessions" facilitated by the most ill-equipped "trainees." This is unfortunate but true. A few horror stories have surfaced from people who went to receive what they thought was to be a Theophostic Ministry session and were hurt even more as a consequence. I am happy to say that of all the thousands of e-mails we receive, only a very small number are negative. Almost all of the negative reports come from unfortunate situations where people simply did not follow the training guidelines and basic principles. However, if research could be obtained concerning any other form of ministry or counseling, you would find the same negative reports surfacing.

Questions to Ask

If you desire authentic Theophostic Ministry, you need to be able to discern whether the person ministering to you is following the basic principles outlined in the Basic Training Seminar. Now and then we have people call in and complain that what they received in a Theophostic Ministry session did not work. In every case we have discovered either a person trying to do Theophostic Ministry who was ill-equipped to do so or someone who was not following the principles as they are taught. What follow are some questions you may want to ask of the person offering Theophostic Ministry before submitting to his or her care.

Will you be guiding or directing the process? People trained in the Theophostic principles are taught *not* to tell you where to go in your memories, not ask leading questions, or tell you what you should experience. This process is God directed and God enlightened. Jesus does not need our insight or help in setting people free from their lies. He allows us to participate in the journey by leading a person to the place where he or she is able to receive, but the transmission of truth must come from Him alone.

Do you use any form of directed imagery or guided visualization? Jesus will reveal truth to you in whatever form He chooses. You may have little to no visualization in this process, which is fine. No one should tell you what you will see or if you will see anything. The one doing ministry with you should not suggest imagery to you. For example, a person should not ask Jesus to do anything for you in the process, such as hold you, take you out of the painful memory, or have Him put the pain in a box or take it away. This is not Theophostic Ministry. However, the minister may ask Jesus questions that are reflective of what you are seeing or experiencing, or may simply ask Him what He wants to do in the memory context. For example, if you reported that you were feeling alone and abandoned, the facilitator might ask Jesus, "What do You want her to know in this memory about why she feels this way?" If you describe a scene where something is happening, the facilitator might ask the Lord, "Is there something in this memory that she still needs to see, understand, or feel?" If you are having a hard time discerning what you believe in the memory, the facilitator might ask Jesus, "What is it in this memory that she believes that is causing her this pain?" When the way is not clear or you do not know what to do, asking Jesus for guidance, direction, or clarity is the right thing to do.

Will you be telling me what you believe is happening during the session? If you are in the memory, the person doing ministry should only help you discern the lies and invite Jesus to reveal His truth. No one should tell you what he or she thinks God wants you to know. The minister's job is to help you reach the place where you are able to discern the lie you are believing and feel its pain, but then the minister should step aside and invite Jesus to reveal the truth you need.

Will you be asking me leading questions or statements? If the minister has an idea or thinks he knows about what may have happened to you, he or she should never suggest it or ask questions that cause you to think in any direction other than what your mind has revealed to you. As mentioned previously, asking questions of you or of Jesus is perfectly acceptable, as long as the questions are reflective of what has been revealed by you the recipient and not the insight or thinking of the facilitator. To ask questions about that which has not been surfaced by you would be to mislead and possibly misdirect the process.

In addition to the above questions, you might want to ask these background questions before you go through a session with a new facilitator.

- Have you been through the Basic Video Training Seminar, which includes watching all video sessions and having read the entire four hundred–plus pages of training materials?
- Are you using the Theophostic principles as your primary means of ministry? (Be careful of those who are mixing other approaches with Theophostic Ministry. If they are, ask if they are using any forms of creative imagery, hypnosis, visualization, or other counselor-directive methods. I am not suggesting that other forms of ministry are not effective, because some are. For example, Neil Anderson's "Steps to Freedom" are excellent and work well with Theophostic Ministry. You will need to decide what you want if the one offering you ministry is using other approaches along with Theophostic Ministry.)
- To how many people have you ministered Theophostic principles where you saw significant freedom using this approach? (Everyone has to start with their first person. The question is, do you want to be their first?)
- Have you experienced healing yourself with this process, and are you continuing this healing? (Something is wrong if the person isn't receiving healing him- or herself and submitting to ministry. We all need this ministry. Those who have received ministry are usually better at ministering to others.)
- Have you continued your study beyond the Basic Seminar materials by attending the advanced training since 1999?

(This advanced training is optional but helpful if dealing with more complex issues. If the minister's training occurred before 1999, he or she does not have the latest information available. If the minister is not trained at the advanced level, however, he or she still may be very effective with most issues.)

- Are you under the authority and spiritual covering of a recognized ministry, church, or professional Christian organization? (If the person is operating as a "lone wolf," be careful. Check out his or her ministry through other established ministries in the area, if possible. Ask for references from those in the area who can give a positive endorsement.)

Be responsible to pray about and discern those from whom you seek ministry. If at any point you feel uncomfortable with what is happening, simply stop the session and decide what it is you need or desire from the person doing the ministry.

On the following page is a copy of an evaluation form we supply to people who call us wanting to know about people in their area doing Theophostic Ministry and a copy of the basic guidelines of a Theophostic ministry session (see end of this book). We encourage those seeking ministry to carefully check out those who are offering ministry before they submit to a session. Never assume that people offering ministry necessarily know what they are doing, or that they are doing Theophostic Ministry simply because they say they are. If you go to a person who is claiming to be using Theophostic Ministry, feel free to make a copy of this form and have him or her complete it before your first session. This will give you some measure of assurance that the counselor is at least on the right page before you begin.

A PREMINISTRY EVALUATION

It is my desire to receive ministry from someone who is trained in the principles of Theophostic Ministry. I <u>do not</u> want any other form of ministry, and desire to be assured that this will not happen in our ministry sessions. Will you please complete this evaluation before we begin? Thank you.

Minister's name: _____

Date: _____

Ministry name: _____

City Location: _____

1. Have you been through the Basic Video Training Seminar, which includes watching all video sessions and having read the entire 400-plus pages of training materials?
YES [ ] NO [ ]

2. Are you using the Theophostic principles as your primary means of ministry and will you avoid using other forms or methods of counseling while ministering with me?
YES [ ] NO [ ]

3. Will you be avoiding all forms of guided imagery, creative visualization, or suggestive thinking, or leading me to visualize anything that is not my own memory content or derived from my own thinking or from the Holy Spirit? Will you avoid guiding or directing the process through suggestive statements and/or leading questions?
YES [ ] NO [ ]

4. Will you avoid providing your insight or thinking into the process as far as making suggestions as to what you think is going on or what you think may have happened to me in my past?
YES [ ] NO [ ]

5. Will you allow the Holy Spirit to provide the truth I need rather than yourself?
YES [ ] NO [ ]

6. To how many people have you ministered Theophostic principles where they reported significant emotional freedom using this approach?
NONE [ ] 1-3 [ ] 3-5 [ ] 6-10 [ ]
MORE THAN 10 [ ]

7. Have you experienced healing yourself with this process, and are you continuing this healing as a regular practice for your life?
YES [ ] NO [ ]

8. Have you continued your study beyond the Basic Seminar materials by attending the advanced training since 1999?
YES [ ] NO [ ]

9. Are you under the authority and spiritual covering of a recognized ministry, church, or professional organization?
YES [ ] Who?
NO [ ] Please explain:

10. Do you have a problem with my sending in this evaluation along with a separate evaluation of what happens in the ministry session to the Theophostic Ministries home office?
YES [ ] NO [ ] If yes, please explain:

Conclusion

Ifirst offered this information on how to administer the Theophostic principles in a Basic Training Seminar in February 1996. I was caught off guard by what I encountered. I was genuinely excited to share the seminar, with a hope that people would be excited as well. Instead, I was faced with a room full of people with their arms crossed, glaring at me as though I were peddling the latest infomercial product. That was over six years ago. Today there are tens of thousands of people ministering to hundreds of thousands of others who are finding peace and mind renewal all around the world. Oh, there are still people with their arms crossed, and even a few who are speaking out against what I am teaching, but the great majority of people are rejoicing with me as the Spirit of Jesus is setting the captives free.

It is my prayer that you will not be sidetracked by the few dissenters and naysayers but will press on for your own healing and find what God has in store for you. If the emotional pain that you are feeling in your day-to-day walk is coming from lie-based thinking, God wants you to know freedom. Many people come into healing very quickly and experience the peace of Christ just a few moments into the ministry session. However, sometimes the process is long, laborious, and excruciating. Still, the peace of God that awaits those who persevere is far beyond comparison to the difficulty of the journey.

Also know that mind renewal is a lifelong, twofold process. It is first the process of our lies being exposed and our willingness to follow our pain to its memory source and find experiential truth, and also the discipleship of diligent self-effort in being filled up with God's Word, so that the "word of Christ [may] richly dwell within you" (Col 3:16). We must come to know God both "cranially" and experientially.

Completing a course of study and offering effective ministry are not always the same. I strongly encourage you to ask many questions of the one from whom you seek ministry. Do not assume that just because a person calls him- or herself a Theophostic minister (which he or she cannot legally do anyway) that the person is capable. Use good judgment, "test the spirits," and ask for references from others who are willing to share with you their own experiences they had with the one offering ministry. Even though there are tens of thousands of people worldwide facilitating Theophostic Ministry, it may be difficult to find a qualified person near you.

If you are unable to locate a qualified person, you may want to encourage those whom you know who are already doing other effective forms of ministry to become trained in the Theophostic principles. This way the ministry you receive may be from someone you already know and trust.

You can obtain a free introductory tape and other pertinent information and order all the training materials by calling or writing the Theophostic Ministries office or by visiting the ministry's web site.

Theophostic Ministries   www.theophostic.com
P.O. Box 489   e-mail: phostic@kyol.net
Campbellsville, KY 42719
Phone: 270-465-3757

Notes

Introduction

1. Abreaction is physical and emotional pain flooding forth as a person embraces a painful memory. The person will often report physical pain in areas of the body where he or she was hurt during the traumatic event. Often the person will seemingly leave the present and experience emotional and physical pain as though she were actually in the memory itself. If there is dissociation present, the person may even take on the personification of the child and act out the mannerisms of the child while experiencing the memory.

One

The Pain Is Gone—ALL Gone!

1. This example, as are those to follow, is *not* an isolated miracle of healing. As of this writing, tens of thousands of people all around the globe are practicing Theophostic Ministry and reporting the same wonderful results. Nearly one thousand people a month are presently completing the Basic Training Seminar and entering into the work. God is raising up an army to do the work of leading people to the only One who can bring true and lasting peace. God is faithful to do all He said that He would do as we work in concert with Him and release Him to minister according to His will and His ways. This example is not intended to imply that Margaret was completely healed of all her childhood memories. She found peace and resolve in the abuse memories that surfaced in their session. Mind renewal is a lifelong process.

Two

Genuine Recovery Versus Tolerable Recovery

1. *Beyond Tolerable Recovery* is the name of the basic seminar manual one receives when one takes the Basic Training Seminar in Theophostic Ministry.

2. When I use New Testament healing stories to explain different aspects of Theophostic Ministry, I am not equating physical healing with the mind renewal process that occurs in a Theophostic session. The "healing" that occurs in a Theophostic Ministry session is the replacing of lies with truth, whereas physical healing is a different phenomena, based upon its own set of biblical and fundamental principles.

Three

The True Source of Our Emotional Pain

1. Whenever you begin a sentence with the word "you" it is a good indication that you are blaming another person for your own lie-based pain.

2. In the Basic Training Seminar I call this a metamorphic lie. It is a present belief that was true during the actual event but is no longer true in the present state.

3. This is a deceptive cycle that is common in Christian circles. It teaches that when I am *defeated* by some sin I need to *confess* it, *repent* and turn from it, *adjust* my attitude, strategy, and approach to dealing with it, and finally *perform* or try harder.

4. I teach on how to deal with dissociation and repression in the Advanced Theophostic Seminars you can attend if you desire to be equipped in this form of ministry. For information on attending a Basic or Advanced Seminar contact the Theophostic office at 270-465-3757 or www.theophostic.com.

5. Eating disorders have many different lie sources. This lie was simply what was behind her disorder. This issue is dealt with in the Advanced Seminars.

Four

Theophostic Ministry: The Renewing of the Mind

1. Self-forgiveness is an interesting concept that has no biblical support. Many teach that self-forgiveness is important and encourage it, yet there

is no evidence that this is something that God desires we do. I have discovered that when people receive truth from the Holy Spirit in their lie-based memories, they no longer feel a need for self-forgiveness.

2. Performance-based spirituality is any behavior or effort on my part to live out the Christian life by way of self-effort, trying harder, self-determination, or works. What is often described as spiritual or Christian behavior is usually nothing more than what lost persons could produce if they set their mind to it. True spiritual living is the effortless outflow of "Christ in me" that occurs as I am able to walk in perfect peace as a result of my mind being renewed to match my inner righteousness.

Five

When God Heals ...

1. Anorexia is a very serious condition that can be life threatening, and it should be dealt with in concert with a medical professional.

2. The opposite of this would be performance-based spirituality.

3. Am I saying we do not need to keep the commandments? Not at all. I am saying that I strive to keep the commandments not so I might be made right or even to avoid being sinful, but rather because I am presently holy and righteous, and doing otherwise is not befitting saints (Eph. 5:3). (The Greek word translated as "saints" in the New Testament is *hagio*, which means simply "holy" or "holy ones."

Six

Releasing Those Who Have Hurt Us

1. Some people don't believe that SRA exists. I would invite these people to spend a few thousand hours in the trenches with these people, as I have over the last few years, to walk with them through their agonizing memories, and to witness the Lord Jesus restoring them. People who lack experience in these areas of ministry are quick to come to wrong conclusions based on unfounded opinions rather than on the "sweat and tears" of doing the work of ministry. I give logical evidence for SRA

in the book *Keeping Your Ministry Out of Court,* which I coauthored with Dr. E. James Wilder.

Seven

Answers to Common Questions About Theophostic Ministry

1. This fellow came up with this when he read a quote from the Basic Seminar Manual in chapter two, on page 38 in the second paragraph. I am explaining how the principles began to come together in my mind and use the analogy of a spigot opening up in my mind and my understanding what I had not before. I would use the same analogy if I were to describe the many times I have gained insight into the Scriptures when preparing for a sermon. There is a big difference between receiving insight into God's Word and receiving a new revelation from God. Insight I have had, divine revelation I have not.

2. It might be possible for an unwise counselor to make a false suggestion in the context of a person's real pain that was coming from a true traumatic memory source. In this context the victim might attach this suggested explanation to the pain he or she was feeling. I actually believe that in most cases, however, the victim will reject such suggestions, since he or she will already know the truth of what happened at a subconscious level. This is one of the reasons why Theophostic Ministry teaches that *no* suggestions as to memory content are ever suggested, all leading questions are avoided, and any hint of visualization or guided imagery is forbidden. People must be allowed to make their own discoveries concerning what has happened to them.

   I am coauthoring a book with Dr. E. James Wilder to help ministers stay within legal boundaries when ministering. One of the areas of our discussion deals with the absurdity of the false memory concept. If you would like to read further on this subject I would encourage you to contact the Theophostic office for details of its publication.

3. Ed Smith, *Beyond Tolerable Recovery: Basic Seminar Manual* (Campbellsville, Ky.: Alathia Publishing, 1999), 18-21.

Theophostic Ministry Facilitator Guidelines

As the facilitator in this Theophostic Ministry session...

- I will avoid all forms of guided imagery and or directed visualization and seek to allow you to have a genuine healing experience that is directed by the Holy Spirit

- I will not make *any* suggestions as to what I think your memory content may contain. I will avoid making suggestions as to what I assume your lie-based thinking may be and thus allow you to make this discovery yourself while relying on the Holy Spirit.

- I will only ask questions that are reflective of the actual memory content or other pertinent information that you alone have surfaced.

- I will not attempt to interpret any information that you surface, for example, dreams, visions, etc. However, I will encourage you to discern the emotions behind these inner-mind realities and seek to find their true memory source.

- I will ask questions to help you discern the lies you may believe in your memories. For example, if you say, "I feel all alone and abandoned." I might ask, "Why do you feel all alone?" You may reply, "Because they all left me." I might say, "Why do you think they left you?" You might respond, "Because they hate me?" I might ask, "Why do you believe that they hate you?" You might say, "Because I am worthless and no good?" etc.

- I will not make any judgments as to whether what you have remembered is true or false but rather seek to help you to discover what is the source of your emotional pain in the context of the memory you have surfaced. I will allow you to come to your own conclusions in your own time concerning the content of your memories.

- I will not supply you with what that I may think God wants you to know during the ministry session itself. I will keep my "words of knowledge or wisdom" to myself until you have arrived at perfect peace in your memory as a result of your receiving truth from the Holy Spirit. I will defer my opinions and thinking to the Spirit of Christ, trusting Him to provide you with His truth and only use my words of insight for confirmation.

- I will ask the Lord Jesus to help you to remember what you have the capacity to embrace and to help you discern the lies you believe that are contained in these memories. Example: "Lord Jesus, will you help (name) to find the place where this emotional pain originated?" "Jesus, what is it you want (name) to know in this memory?" "Will you help (name) to know what she/he believes in this memory that is not true?" "Will you help (name) to discover what is causing her to feel the pain she feels?" etc.

- I will be careful to discern and call attention to anything that surfaces which does not appear to be authentic and or biblically consistent. Should this happen, we will work together to determine what is true or not and where such information originated.

- Should I have some visual picture appear in my mind that I believe is related to your memory, I will not report this to you lest I implant ideas into your thinking. You do not need my personal insight to find the truth that the Holy Spirit has for you. Should your experience cause me to see images or pictures, I will keep them to myself.

- I will do my best not to hinder your healing by inputting my personal assumptions, insight, or thinking that is directive or leading in nature. My desire is that you have a genuine encounter with the Spirit of Christ. He alone is the only one who can truly release you of the emotional lie-based pain in your life.

Training Materials for Theophostic Ministry

■ **Basic Training Seminar Package**

The core materials for Basic training in Theophostic Ministry. This package includes the video sessions of training, Basic Seminar Manual, Video Workbook, Facilitator's guide and Ministry Orientation Manual.

■ **"Genuine Recovery" Ministry Orientation Manual**

The Orientation Manual provides orientation for the one receiving ministry so they may better understand the Theophostic process. When the one receiving ministry comprehends the basic principles the sessions tend to be more productive and exhibit less resistance. This manual should be provided for each person who receives ministry through the Theophostic process. Those people who supply this manual to those with whom they minister, report great benefit. Included with the Basic Training Package listed above.

■ **Basic Ingredients For a Happy Marriage**

This series is a six-cassette tape set designed to strengthen the marriage or prepare the engaged couple for a successful marriage. Dr. Ed and Sharon Smith provide a humorous yet insightful look at such issues as Discovering How to Live With Male and Female Differences, Learning to Meet the Love Needs of Your Mate, Sexual Fulfillment in Marriage, Developing Communication Skills, and Understanding each Other.

Other Ministry Tools From Theophostic Ministries

■ **Facilitator's Ministry Session Flip Chart**

A "desktop" full-color flip chart presentation of all the primary principles of Theophostic Ministry includes the basic principles, understanding memory, dissociation and repression, and more. This tool is to be used in the actual ministry session to better educate the ministry recipient in Theophostic Ministry.

■ Trouble Shooter's Guide to Theophostic Ministry

This tool is a comprehensive guide designed to provide possible solutions to the reasons for some of the barriers and hindrances encountered during a ministry session. It is presented in a "If this happens.... try this" format. It has a comprehensive index and table of contents for easy access of information.

■ Keeping Your Ministry Out of Court: Avoiding Unnecessary Litigation While Ministering to Emotionally Wounded People

This is a MUST BUY book for those using Theophostic Ministry. If you believe you could never be sued for ministering in the name of Christ, wake up! If you are ministering to hurting people you are a candidate for satanic sabotage and possible lawsuit. Ed M. Smith and E. James Wilder offer a means by which ministers and counselors can answer God's call and offer care to the emotionally wounded person while being "wise as serpents" and avoiding unnecessary litigation.

■ International Association for Theophostic Ministry

Become a member of what may soon become one of the world's largest Christian ministry associations. Join a network of thousands of people worldwide using the Theophostic principles in ministry and in their own personal lives. Participate in international TPM conferences, conventions, and other training events as well as stay informed with the tri-annual TPM Journal. Contact the Theophostic Ministry office for membership details (270-789-0220) or visit the web site at www.tpassociation.com.

■ Theophostic Ministry Advanced Training Video Seminar

Twelve-tape video series dealing with advanced issues in Theophostic Ministry. Participants must meet special requirements to participate in this training. Contact the Theophostic Ministries office for details (270-465-3757) (www.theophostic.com).

For More Information Contact Theophostic Ministries
270-465-3757 or www.theophostic.com